I0102395

Choosing Democracy

Not Old Enough to Vote: Old Enough to Lead

ABIGAIL SAXEN

Choosing Democracy

Copyright © 2026 by Abigail Saxen.

All rights reserved. No part of this publication may be reproduced, distributed, or transmitted in any form or by any means, including photocopying, recording, or other electronic or mechanical methods, without the written consent of the publisher. The only exceptions are for brief quotations included in critical reviews and other noncommercial uses permitted by copyright law.

MILTON & HUGO L.L.C.
1001 3rd Avenue West, Suite 430
Bradenton, FL 34205, USA

Website: *www. miltonandhugo.com*
Hotline: *1- 888-778-0033*
Email: *info@miltonandhugo.com*

Ordering Information:
Quantity sales. Special discounts are granted to corporations, associations, and other organizations. For more information on these discounts, please reach out to the publisher using the contact information provided above.

ISBN-13:	979-8-89285-273-9	[Paperback Edition]
	979-8-89285-274-6	[Hardback Edition]
	979-8-89285-272-2	[Digital Edition]

Rev. date: 01/28/2026

Dedicated to those who are unable to write freely without persecution.
I hope that someday the world will get to hear your ideas.

CONTENTS

INTRODUCTION

Unless. "Unless someone like you cares a whole awful lot, nothing is going to get better. It's not."-Dr. Seuss. On a cold January morning in 2021, the world watched in disbelief as the U.S. Capitol, which had been a symbol of democratic resilience, was stormed by its own citizens in opposition to a peaceful transition of power. For some, it was a wake-up call; for others, it was a sign of deeper decay. But the unraveling of democracy does not begin with shattered windows and chaos. It begins in quieter places, like a school board meeting where dissent is silenced, a law redrawing voting maps in the shadows, or a legal action taken without due process. These are the small fractures that, left unchecked, grow into collapse. Democracy is not a fortress. It is a flame-powerful, illuminating, and vulnerable to neglect. The question now is not whether democracy *can* survive, but whether we will do the work to preserve it. This book is about that work. It is about students who protest, voters who elect politicians that speak up against unjust laws, and citizens who fight for systems that uphold inalienable rights, for everyone. Each chapter offers a step forward and a reason to believe the flame can still be kept alive. To fight to keep the flame alive. Because democracies do not die in darkness. They die in daylight, while we are busy looking the other way. Let us choose, then, to look closer. Let us choose to act. Let us choose to keep the flame burning.

BELIEF PERSEVERANCE

Historically, all American political parties have contributed to corruption or weakening of democracy in some way. Recently, both the Democratic and Republican parties have contributed to losses of freedom. Yet, a Democrat would most likely tell you that the Trump administration was the sole cause of this loss, while a Republican would probably say that the Biden administration is the only responsible party. The likelihood of either of these statements being true is nonzero, but nonetheless very low. In general, absolute statements lack validity.

Almost every American is alert and cautious about presidential elections, and perhaps worried about the outcome and the future of the country. It is very easy to view the success of the candidate from the opposite party as a threat to democracy and freedom. Most people have beliefs that are aligned with one of the two most prominent political parties in the U.S. Most people continue to be astonished that members of the opposite party could ever believe what they believe. I do not blame anyone for that, as I have experienced this myself, but I would encourage every American to keep a few things in mind as we continue to live in an era where politics is extremely polarized.

The number one factor of political socialization is the political views of one's family.[1] In other words, what your parents believe is likely what you will believe as well. When a person has associated themselves with a political party, it is highly unlikely that they will change their beliefs, beliefs that have likely come from their parents. This makes it very difficult to have productive conversations with people about politics; normally, people have political conversations with members

---

[1] Longley, Robert. "What Is Political Socialization? Definition and Examples." ThoughtCo, 3 Mar. 2021, www.thoughtco.com/political-socialization-5104843.

of the opposite party to talk, not to listen. I understand that it may be challenging to actually listen to what people from the opposite party have to say. I find it difficult to listen to opposing views for the purpose of understanding the other side, rather than for the purpose of criticizing and judging the other side. But this does not get us anywhere.

In recent years, American politics has become more and more of an entertainment industry. There are two major problems with this. Firstly, this development has caused hyperpolarization. Just like reality television, it becomes increasingly animating to pick a side and become a die-hard member of that side. Especially during a presidential election year, politics becomes such a big part of almost every media outlet. However, I would warn us against this. We have forgotten that from the founding of this country, the goal of politics and the government has not been to create entertainment for its citizens. It has not been to divide its citizens into pieces. It has not been to form an "us versus them" mentality among almost every single American. It has been to provide a unifying and mediating force for its citizens, and to protect our rights and freedoms. That does not seem to be the case anymore, but I am confident that it can be again.

Second, this development also takes away any hope of mediation. The presidential debates of 2024 are a perfect example of this. Most Americans who watched these debates watched them with the purpose of laughing about how unintelligent the candidate of the opposing party sounded, and not to find out more about the candidates' views.[2] Very few people watched them with the originally intended purpose: listening to both candidates in order to notice which person had the better ideas. If the former is the reason for your viewing of the debate, you are not alone. As previously mentioned, I am guilty of this as well. And as fun as it was to watch these debates with the purpose of entertainment, it is not productive, and it is not what politics is for.

Politics will never be completely free of belief perseverance, but there are steps that citizens can take to mitigate its negative effects. To start, do not automatically believe everything you read in this book. I write

---

[2]   DeSilver, Drew. "6 Facts about Presidential and Vice Presidential Debates." Pew Research Center, 21 June 2024, www.pewresearch.org/short-reads/2024/06/21/6-facts-about-presidential-and-vice-presidential-debates/.

to share what is generally proven to keep democracy alive by providing thought provoking facts and analysis. I do not write to convince you that my words are the absolute truth. Given the same facts, someone could write a completely different analysis. Of course, I would encourage you to consider my analysis; I would not be writing this book if I did not. However, come up with your own as well. Question everything, and do your own research. Talk to people with different opinions. Read multiple perspectives. Never settle on an absolute opinion. Until the 1840s, people thought that the shape of someone's head could determine their entire personality. Until the early 1800s, it was believed that lead could be spun into gold. Until the late 1600s, people believed that lambs grew on trees. The point is, humans have been getting things wrong for hundreds of thousands of years. It is part of the process of discovery. It is great to be wrong, because it sets up the pathway for progress. But it only leads to progress if you continually look for new evidence and ideas. The following list is a guide to help avoid belief perseverance, because no one in the world is immune to it. Following these steps will not eliminate it, but it will help mitigate it and make you aware of it in your thoughts and in the actions of others.

Accept the Infallibility of No One

For most people, it is clear to see that the people we know personally make tons of mistakes. And they are wrong, a lot. For some reason, though, the electorate in the United States(and worldwide) has a habit of putting politicians on a pedestal, and thinking that they can do no wrong. Of course, if a particular politician is from the opposite party from you, you may think that they can do no right. It is not the mistakes of politicians that are dangerous. It is the notion of infallibility among their supporters. Currently, President Donald Trump supporters are the most well-known example of this, and for good reason. The Trump administration has made colossal mistakes. It texted highly confidential war plans to a wrong number, temporarily crashed the global economy due to the tariffs it implemented, deported people who were in the country legally, and still retains the support of its most loyal voters. It is not the continual support of Trump that is most concerning, though.

To be completely fair, the administration quickly reduced most of the tariffs after the global economy declined. What is concerning, is that many, if not most, of Trump's supporters believe that these tariffs were never a mistake, and that the Trump administration did not do anything wrong. It is not all Trump supporters that believe this, but it is enough to cause worry.

This issue is quite clear to anyone that leans left. However, this is an issue among the left-wing part of the electorate as well. President Barack Obama led the United States for eight years, and made several mistakes throughout. For example, the Obama administration's exit from the Republic of Iraq in 2011 caused ISIS, a violent terrorist organization, to grow in Iraq and led to the death or suffering of many Iraqi citizens.[3] As a general trend, members of the Republican party correctly recognize this decision as a huge mistake, while members of the Democratic party either dismiss it or attempt to justify the incident. Of course, not all members of either party dismiss mistakes that politicians they support have made, but it is enough for all of us to reflect on our own belief perseverance.

In fact, let us look at two blunders from each party: Obama's Iraq exit and Trump's tariffs. 8% of Democrats disapproved of Obama's decision to pull out of Iraq by the end of 2011, while a significantly higher 47% of Republicans disapproved.[4] Conversely, an opinion poll taken shortly after the tariffs were implemented found that 96% of Democrats disapproved of Trump's handling of the tariffs, while only 25% of Republicans disapproved.[5] A limitation of this comparison is that Obama's exit from Iraq had broad support while Trump's tariffs had broad disapproval. Obama's decision was largely deemed a blunder

---

[3] White, Jeremy B. "How the Obama Administration Ignored Iraq." POLITICO Magazine, 2 Oct. 2014, www.politico.com/magazine/story/2014/10/how-the-obama-administration-disowned-iraq-111565/. Accessed 6 June 2025.

[4] NW, 1615 L. St, et al. "Section 4: Views of Iraq." Pew Research Center - U.S. Politics & Policy, 17 Nov. 2011, www.pewresearch.org/politics/2011/11/17/section-4-views-of-iraq/.

[5] Ishai Melamede. "Nearly Two-Thirds of Americans Disapprove of Trump Tariffs, with Inflation a Broad Concern: POLL." ABC News, 25 Apr. 2025, abcnews.go.com/Politics/thirds-americans-disapprove-trump-tariffs-inflation-broad-concern/story?id=121123815.

in retrospect, after this particular poll was taken. Nonetheless, most experts agree that both of these policies were mistakes.[6] Yet, belief perseverance and partisanship influenced the ability of citizens to hold our politicians accountable, because no one is infallible.

The burden to hold politicians, especially presidents, cannot continue to fall on just half of the citizens. During President Joseph Biden's presidency, the burden to hold him accountable was put almost entirely on Republicans, and during Trump's presidency, the burden is almost fully on Democrats. It takes all of us, not just certain political parties, and not just the electorate. As of when I am writing this, I have never voted in an election because I am not old enough. Yet, I work toward accountability in other ways by volunteering and canvassing for causes I believe in, and by keeping myself informed by trustworthy and multi-partisan sources. Making a difference beyond voting will be discussed more in depth later.

Allow New Evidence To Change Your Beliefs (Even More Than Once)

As a child, I fully believed that at any moment the Earth could start falling down in space. The reason I thought this was because I was pulling from a database in which that event occurring was a real possibility. Things did not simply float in air; they fell to the ground if they were not resting on a surface. I had not taken physics yet, and I did not know how gravity really worked. So I assumed gravity was always a downward force rather than an attractive force, because "stuff falling down" was all I had ever known and witnessed it to be. Then, when I learned about orbits, I expanded my understanding of gravity to include objects' attraction to each other, and not just things falling down. I changed my beliefs in light of new information.

---

6   Greenhouse, Steven. "Economists Agree: Trump Is Wrong on Tariffs." The Century Foundation, 31 Jan. 2025, tcf.org/content/commentary/economists-agree-trump-is-wrong-on-tariffs/.
Traub, James. "The Mess Obama Left behind in Iraq." Foreign Policy, 7 Oct. 2016, foreignpolicy.com/2016/10/07/the-mess-obama-left-behind-in-iraq-surge-debate/.

This concept, called accommodation[7] in psychology, can be applied to politics. Let us look at an example. Say Alex, a twenty-eight-year-old software engineer from a small Midwestern town, firmly believed that government welfare programs mostly encouraged laziness and dependency. Growing up, he had seen a few neighbors misuse food stamps and disability checks, and in his view, they never seemed to make any effort to find jobs. To him, this personal experience confirmed what he often heard in casual conversation, that welfare was broken and abused. One day, during a workplace training on data analysis, a colleague used a real-world dataset to demonstrate visualization tools. The dataset included information from the U.S. Census Bureau and Department of Labor on welfare usage, employment rates, and transitions off public assistance. Alex began digging deeper.

He discovered that the overwhelming majority of welfare recipients were either working low-wage jobs, actively seeking employment, or temporarily out of work due to disability or caregiving responsibilities. The data also showed that most people used welfare as a short-term support, not a long-term crutch. Studies indicated that programs like SNAP and Medicaid actually improved long-term employment outcomes and child health. Confronted with broad, peer-reviewed data that contradicted his anecdotal impressions, Alex reconsidered his belief. He realized that while his personal experiences were valid, they were not representative. The bigger picture was far more complex than he had assumed.

Alex now has a better understanding of this issue, and so he corrects his thinking. However, the only facts that can be gathered from this story are that he previously had a narrow understanding of this topic, and then later expanded his knowledge and improved his understanding. It is possible and likely that there is an even bigger and more generalizable set of data that Alex has not yet come across. Just because he expanded his understanding does not mean that it is the widest it can be; in fact, it is near impossible that it is, given how much knowledge exists in the world, discovered or not. This is why it is so important to constantly keep

[7] Mcleod, Saul. "Accommodation and Assimilation in Psychology - Simply Psychology." Www.simplypsychology.org, 24 Jan. 2024, www.simplypsychology. org/what-is-accommodation-and-assimilation.html.

an open mind and be looking to learn new information. If you changed your mind about a belief due to new evidence and critical thinking, that is great, but this does not mean that your new belief is now the absolute truth. In order to have the best possible understanding of a political issue, you should not only allow your opinion to be changed by new evidence, but you should constantly be in search of it.

Avoid Group Polarization

This involves yet another psychological concept. Group polarization occurs when individuals discuss a topic for which they have similar opinions, and each person ends up with a more extreme version of the opinion they previously had.[8] Let us look outside the United States to an infamous and brutal example of group polarization in politics: the 1994 Rwandan genocide. Leading up to the genocide, political discourse between the Hutu majority and the Tutsi minority became increasingly polarized. What began as ethnic and political differences intensified through group polarization and echo chambers, particularly via the extremist radio station Radio Télévision Libre des Mille Collines (RTLM).[9] Many Hutu people disliked the Tutsi people because of deep rooted ethnic tension, which was exacerbated by German and then Belgian colonial rule.[10] The RTLM caused group polarization among its listeners, because it made their negative opinions about the Tutsi people more extreme by affirming and echoing them. Over eight hundred thousand Rwandans, primarily Tutsi people, were killed in the span of just one hundred days.[11]

---

[8] The University of Texas Permian Basin. "Lost in the Crowd: The Phenomenon of Group Polarization | UT Permian Basin Online." Online.utpb.edu, 10 Oct. 2022, online.utpb.edu/about-us/articles/psychology/lost-in-the-crowd-the-phenomenon-of-group-polarization/.

[9] Lyon, Meghan. "Radio in the Rwandan Genocide - the Devil's Tale." The Devil's Tale, 1 May 2017, blogs.library.duke.edu/rubenstein/2013/05/10/radio-in-the-rwandan-genocide/.

[10] Braeckman, Colette. "Belgium's Role in Rwandan Genocide." Le Monde Diplomatique, 1 June 2021, mondediplo.com/2021/06/11rwanda.

[11] BBC News. "Rwanda: How the Genocide Happened." BBC News, 17 May 2011, www.bbc.com/news/world-africa-13431486.

It would be naive to say that group polarization in the United States could currently cause this level of violence. However, it would be naive to say that this genocide is an isolated evil and that it will never happen again in the history of the world. Already in human history, this level of genocide has occured against multiple people groups, countries, and time periods.[12] Group polarization at this level is responsible for the murder of millions. On a more common level, it undermines democracy and personal freedoms, even slightly. For example, it is likely one of the primary causes of gridlock in both houses of the U.S. Congress, which often prevents key legislation that would be beneficial to many Americans from being passed. Unfortunately, it is difficult for individual citizens to control the actions of Senators and House Representatives. What we can do is work to minimize the effects of group polarization in politics on an individual level. The people of a democracy set the precedent for the political culture, not the politicians.

There are five main steps to mitigate the negative impact of group polarization on democracy. First, seek cross-cutting dialogue. Engage with people who hold different political or ideological views. Exposure to multiple perspectives challenges assumptions and reduces echo chambers. Second, practice active listening and critical thinking. Rather than reacting emotionally or defensively, question how and why you hold certain beliefs. Is it based on data, or just repeated narratives within your group? Third, diversify your information sources. Relying only on ideologically aligned news or social media reinforces bias. Reading from a broad spectrum of sources helps avoid one-sided thinking. Fourth, encourage internal dissent within your own group. Respectful disagreement within a group prevents echo chambers. Leaders and members should welcome constructive criticism and opposing viewpoints. Fifth, slow down the decision-making process. Polarization often escalates in fast-paced environments. Taking time to reflect allows for more rational, less emotionally driven conclusions. Individuals following these steps could change the unproductive aspects of political

---

[12] The Wiener Holocaust Library. "Genocides." The Wiener Holocaust Library, 2021, wienerholocaustlibrary.org/what-we-do/learn/subject-guides/genocides/.

ABIGAIL SAXEN

culture in the U.S. and enhance democracy. Everyone following these steps could prevent an unknowable amount of deaths.

Consume Quality News

No matter what your political party is, or if you do not align with either party, make sure your news is from a reliable source. All sources are biased in some way, so rather than worrying about getting your news from the least partisan source possible, get your information from a variety of sources that are from different ends of the political spectrum. Most Republican news sources do not publish errors made by Republican politicians, and most Democratic news sources do not publish errors made by Democratic politicians. Getting your news from a variety of sources ensures that you are informed and able to hold all politicians accountable, even the ones you support.

In a world in which social media is a big part of life, this is especially important. Social media is a catalyst for political polarization, and of course, yellow journalism. The algorithm is designed to show you videos that align with your beliefs. Always fact check what you hear on social media. I know that may seem obvious, but it can be difficult to remember that some news may be false or exaggerated, especially when the creator seems to be informed, and when they hold similar beliefs to you. Be extra cautious about posts that are attempting to invoke fear, anger, or sadness in its viewers. This type of content gets the most engagement, and most of the time real life is not interesting enough to go viral. Always be sure to corroborate reliable sources if you hear "facts" about politics from social media.

A SHORT HISTORY OF AUTHORITARIAN REGIMES: PARALLELS WITH THE CONTEMPORARY U.S.

"History doesn't repeat itself, but it often rhymes."-Mark Twain. Let us look at some parallels between the current political situation in the United States and different events in history. The following list, starting with Argentina, compares stories of democratically elected leaders that have gradually turned into dictatorships with the current way that the United States is operating. While it is not likely that the U.S. will turn into a dictatorship soon, it is crucial to be aware of that fact that democracy is fragile, and to look at historical precedence to ensure that these types of trends do not happen in the U.S. The most important thing to recognize is that, while democracy in the U.S. is currently being threatened by a right-wing presidency, this is just an example. Left-wing presidencies can do just as much damage, and it is just as important to be aware in that situation as well.

United States, 2025

Donald Trump

Trump was democratically elected in 2016 and then again in 2024. Congressman Andy Ogles (R-Tenn.) recently proposed a constitutional amendment that would permit a president to serve up to three terms, provided they have not served two consecutive terms. This proposal is designed to enable Trump to run for another term, as his two terms are non-consecutive. However, the amendment specifies that this rule would not apply to former Presidents Barack Obama, Bill Clinton, or George W. Bush, who each served two consecutive terms.[13]

Argentina, 1976

Military Junta (De Facto Leadership)

Although the dictatorship was led by a military coup against Isabel Perón's government, the democratic instability and abuses of power by elected leaders before the coup contributed to the collapse of democracy.[14]

Belarus, 1994

Alexander Lukashenko

Lukashenko was elected in 1994 in the first democratic presidential election. Over time, he manipulated the constitution, eliminated term limits, and suppressed opposition, turning Belarus into a dictatorship. Belarus is still currently considered to be a dictatorship in 2025.[15]

Bolivia, 2019

Evo Morales

Morales was democratically elected in 2006 and served until 2019. He extended term limits via constitutional changes and controversial

[13] Mangan, Dan. "Constitutional Amendment to Allow Trump Third Term Introduced in the House." CNBC, 24 Jan. 2025, www.cnbc.com/2025/01/23/trump-third-term-amendment-constitution-ogles.html.

[14] Intelligence, Office of the Director of National, and Michael D. Thomas. "INTEL - Argentina Declassification Project: History." Www.intel.gov, www.intel.gov/argentina/history.

[15] Wesolowsky, Tony. "Elections in Belarus: How Lukashenka Won and Won and Won and Won and Won." RadioFreeEurope/RadioLiberty, 5 Aug. 2020, www.rferl.org/a/elections-in-belarus-how-lukashenka-won-and-won-and-won-and-won-and-won-/30767860.html.

elections. Though he resigned amid accusations of fraud, his actions contributed to democratic backsliding.[16]

Cambodia, 1975

Pol Pot

Pol Pot's regime took control after the Khmer Rouge ousted the Cambodian government. Though elections were held, democratic processes were quickly dismantled, leading to a brutal dictatorship.[17]

Central African Republic, 1966

Jean-Bédel Bokassa

Bokassa, originally part of the government, seized power and later declared himself emperor. His regime was marked by authoritarianism and human rights abuses.[18]

El Salvador, 2020

Nayib Bukele

Elected in 2019, Bukele dissolved checks on his power, dismissed Supreme Court judges, and concentrated authority in the executive

---

[16] "Restoring Democracy: Lessons from Bolivia since the 2019 Coupvolution - the SAIS Review of International Affairs." The SAIS Review of International Affairs -, 18 Dec. 2024, saisreview.sais.jhu.edu/restoring-democracy-lessons-from bolivia-since-the-2019-coupvolution/.

[17] https://cla.umn.edu/chgs/holocaust-genocide-education/resource-guides/cambodia

[18] University of Central Arkansas. "36. Central African Republic (1960-Present)." Uca.edu, uca.edu/politicalscience/home/research-projects/dadm-project/sub-saharan-africa-region/central-african-republic-1960-present/.

branch. His government has been accused of using state institutions for authoritarian purposes.[19]

Ethiopia, 2021

Abiy Ahmed

Initially hailed as a reformer after being elected in 2018, Abiy gradually centralized power. His handling of the Tigray conflict, along with restrictions on opposition, has drawn criticism for authoritarian tendencies.[20]

Germany, 1933

Adolf Hitler

Hitler was appointed Chancellor in 1933 after the Nazi Party won significant support in democratic elections. Following the Reichstag Fire, he pushed through the Enabling Act, granting himself dictatorial powers. By 1934, he had abolished all opposition, transforming Germany into a totalitarian state.[21]

---

[19] Smith, Kathleen. "Rising Authoritarianism in El Salvador: What Happens after the Crisis | Fragile States Index." Fragilestatesindex.org, 20 May 2021, fragilestatesindex.org/2021/05/20/rising-authoritarianism-in-el-salvador-what-happens-after-the-crisis/.

[20] Human Rights Watch. "Ethiopia: Events of 2021." Human Rights Watch, 13 Jan. 2022, www.hrw.org/world-report/2022/country-chapters/ethiopia.

[21] United States Holocaust Memorial Museum. "Hitler Comes to Power." Holocaust Encyclopedia, United States Holocaust Memorial Museum, 23 Feb. 2022, encyclopedia.ushmm.org/content/en/article/hitler-comes-to-power.

Haiti, 1957

François "Papa Doc" Duvalier

Duvalier was elected president in 1957 but declared himself president for life in 1964. He ruled through fear, creating a police state and suppressing all opposition.[22]

Honduras, 2009

Manuel Zelaya

Zelaya, elected in 2006, sought to extend his presidential term through constitutional reforms. His actions were deemed unconstitutional, leading to a coup. Although his dictatorship was short-lived, it destabilized Honduras' democracy.[23]

Hungary, 2010

Viktor Orbán

Elected in 2010, Orbán used his parliamentary majority to rewrite the constitution, weaken judicial independence, control the media, and suppress dissent. Hungary is now often described as an "illiberal democracy" or soft authoritarian state.[24]

---

[22] The Editors of Encyclopaedia Britannica. "François Duvalier | President of Haiti | Britannica." Encyclopædia Britannica, 2019, www.britannica.com/biography/Francois-Duvalier.

[23] Fernandez, Belen. "Memories of a Honduran Coup." Www.aljazeera.com, 28 June 2021, www.aljazeera.com/opinions/2021/6/28/memories-of-a-honduran-coup.

[24] Bozóki, András. "The Politics of Worst Practices: Hungary in the 2010s." Les Dossiers Du CERI, 10 Feb. 2015, www.sciencespo.fr/ceri/fr/content/dossiersduceri/politics-worst-practices-hungary-2010s.

Indonesia, 1967

Suharto

Suharto, initially elected as a leader under Sukarno's government, consolidated power through a "New Order" regime, dismantling democratic institutions and ruling with authoritarian control until 1998.[25]

Iraq, 1958

Abdul Karim Qasim

Following the overthrow of the monarchy, Qasim rose to power. Initially framed as a democratic shift, Qasim consolidated power and suppressed opposition, leading to authoritarian rule.[26]

Italy, 1925

Benito Mussolini

Mussolini became Prime Minister in 1922 after his party gained parliamentary seats. By 1925, he dismantled democratic institutions, banned opposition parties, and declared himself dictator, creating a fascist regime.[27]

---

[25] History.com Editors. "Suharto Takes Full Power in Indonesia | February 22, 1967 | HISTORY." HISTORY, 21 July 2010, www.history.com/this-day-in-history/february-22/suharto-takes-full-power-in-indonesia.

[26] Woods, John. "Iraq - the Republic of Iraq." Encyclopedia Britannica, www.britannica.com/place/Iraq/The-Republic-of-Iraq.

[27] History.com Editors. "Benito Mussolini Declares Himself Dictator of Italy | January 3, 1925 | HISTORY." HISTORY, 9 Sept. 2019, www.history.com/this-day-in-history/january-3/benito-mussolini-declares-himself-dictator-of-italy.

Ivory Coast, 2011

Laurent Gbagbo

Gbagbo was elected president but refused to step down after losing the 2010 election. This triggered a violent crisis, and although he was eventually ousted, his actions weakened the country's democratic framework.[28]

Kenya, 1969 and 1982

Jomo Kenyatta 1969

After independence, Kenya's multiparty democracy was dismantled. Kenyatta banned opposition in 1969.[29]

Daniel arap Moi 1982

Moi declared Kenya a one-party state in 1982, leading to decades of authoritarian rule.[30]

Malaysia, 1969

Tunku Abdul Rahman

The government declared a state of emergency after ethnic riots in 1969, suspending parliament and consolidating power. This led to

---

[28] Essa, Azad. "Ivory Coast: The Brink of Civil War." Www.aljazeera.com, 2011, www.aljazeera.com/news/2011/12/27/ivory-coast-the-brink-of-civil-war.

[29] Ajulu, Rok. "Kenya: The Road to Democracy." Review of African Political Economy, no. 53, 1992, pp. 79–87. JSTOR, www.jstor.org/stable/4005993, https://doi.org/10.2307/4005993.

[30] Princeton University. "Kenya 1982." Princeton.edu, 2025, pcwcr.princeton.edu/reports/kenya1982.html. Accessed 3 June 2025.

decades of dominance by the ruling coalition, with limited democratic competition.[31]

Maldives, 1978

Maumoon Abdul Gayoom

Gayoom was elected through single-party systems and maintained control for three decades. Elections were tightly controlled, ensuring his grip on power.[32]

Nicaragua, 2007

Daniel Ortega

Ortega was initially elected in 1984, left office, and returned to power in 2007. Over time, he dismantled democratic institutions, restricted press freedom, suppressed dissent, and manipulated elections to maintain his rule.[33]

Paraguay, 1954

Alfredo Stroessner

Stroessner was democratically elected but soon declared a state of emergency and ruled as a dictator for thirty-five years. He used the military, repression, and constitutional changes to maintain power.[34]

---

[31] Parmer, J. Norman. "Malaysia 1965: Challenging the Terms of 1957." Asian Survey, vol. 6, no. 2, 1 Feb. 1966, pp. 111–118, https://doi.org/10.2307/2642106. Accessed 8 Mar. 2021.

[32] University of Central Arkansas. "41. Maldives (1965-Present)." Uca.edu, uca.edu/politicalscience/home/research-projects/dadm-project/asiapacific-region/maldives-1965-present/.

[33] "Nicaragua." U.S. Department of State, 2017, 2009-2017.state.gov/j/drl/rls/afdr/2008/wha/129933.htm. Accessed 3 June 2025.

[34] The Editors of Encyclopedia Britannica. "Alfredo Stroessner | President of Paraguay." Encyclopædia Britannica, 30 Oct. 2018, www.britannica.com/biography/Alfredo-Stroessner.

Peru, 1992 and 2022

Alberto Fujimori(1992)[35]

Democratically elected in 1990, Fujimori staged an "autogolpe" (self-coup) in 1992, dissolving Congress and ruling by decree. He maintained authoritarian control, suppressing opposition and media freedom.

Pedro Castillo(2022)[36]

Castillo was elected in 2021, but in December 2022, he attempted to dissolve Congress and rule by decree, leading to his removal. This was seen as an effort to bypass democratic checks and consolidate power.

Philippines, 1972

Ferdinand Marcos

Marcos was elected president in 1965 and reelected in 1969. In 1972, he declared martial law, citing threats to national security. He ruled as a dictator until 1986, using violence, corruption, and electoral fraud to maintain power.[37]

---

[35] Reuters. "Peru Suspends Democracy, Citing Revolt (Published 1992)." New York Times, 7 Apr. 1992, www.nytimes.com/1992/04/07/world/peru-suspends-democracy-citing-revolt.html.

[36] Collyns, Dan. "Peru President Removed from Office amid Accusations of Coup Attempt." The Guardian, 7 Dec. 2022, www.theguardian.com/world/2022/dec/07/peru-president-detained-pedro-castillo-coup.

[37] Britannica. "Philippines - Martial Law." Encyclopædia Britannica, 2019, www.britannica.com/place/Philippines/Martial-law.

Poland, 2015

The Law and Justice Party (PiS) and Jarosław Kaczyński (De Facto Leader)

While Poland remains technically democratic, the PiS government, elected in 2015, undermined judicial independence, suppressed free media, and eroded democratic institutions, moving toward authoritarianism.[38]

Russia, 2000

Vladimir Putin

Initially elected in 2000, Putin centralized power over time. Through constitutional changes, suppression of opposition, and control of media and institutions, he effectively dismantled democratic processes. By 2021, he extended his ability to remain in power until 2036.[39]

Singapore, 1965

Lee Kuan Yew

Elected in 1959, Lee Kuan Yew oversaw Singapore's transition to independence. While his government delivered economic success, it also suppressed dissent, limited free speech, and used the legal system to maintain political dominance, creating a tightly controlled system.[40]

---

[38] Smeltzer, Mike. "Polish Democracy at a Crossroads." Freedom House, 21 Sept. 2023, freedomhouse.org/article/polish-democracy-crossroads.

[39] Savranskaya, Svetlana, et al. "Putin's First Election, March 2000 | National Security Archive." Nsarchive.gwu.edu, 21 Mar. 2024, nsarchive.gwu.edu/briefing-book/russia-programs/2024-03-21/putins-first-election-march-2000.

[40] Kurlantzick, Joshua. "Singapore's Social Contract Is Starting to Fray." Council on Foreign Relations, 23 Aug. 2023, www.cfr.org/article/singapores-social-contract-starting-fray.

South Korea, 1972

Park Chung-hee

Park seized power in a 1961 coup but later won elections in a semi-democratic system. In 1972, he declared martial law, suspended the constitution, and created a dictatorship known as the "Yushin" system.[41]

Sri Lanka, 2020

Gotabaya Rajapaksa

After being elected in 2019, Rajapaksa amended the constitution to expand presidential powers, bypassing parliament. His administration suppressed opposition and dissent, triggering protests and political instability.[42]

Sudan, 2019

Omar al-Bashir

Bashir came to power in a military coup but legitimized his rule through elections. Over time, he consolidated power, suppressed opposition, and created a dictatorship until his ousting in 2019.[43]

---

[41] Im, Hyug-Baeg. "South Korea - the Yushin Order (Fourth Republic)." *Encyclopedia Britannica*, www.britannica.com/place/South-Korea/The-Yushin-order-Fourth-Republic.

[42] "Sri Lanka." *United States Department of State*, www.state.gov/reports/2020-country-reports-on-human-rights-practices/sri-lanka/.

[43] Gavin, Michelle. "Pro-Democracy Movement Persists in Sudan." *Council on Foreign Relations*, 22 June 2022, www.cfr.org/blog/pro-democracy-movement-persists-sudan.

Syria, 1971

Hafez al-Assad

Hafez al-Assad was elected president in 1971 under a one-party system and established a family dynasty. His son, Bashar, continues to rule, suppressing opposition and maintaining a dictatorship.[44]

Tunisia, 2021

Kais Saied

Elected in 2019, Saied dissolved parliament in 2021, ruling by decree and bypassing democratic checks. Critics accused him of orchestrating a coup and moving toward dictatorship.[45]

Turkey, 2017

Recep Tayyip Erdoğan

After being elected in 2003 as Prime Minister and later as President, Erdoğan used a failed coup attempt in 2016 to justify a crackdown on opposition and dissent. In 2017, constitutional reforms transitioned Turkey from a parliamentary to a presidential system, significantly expanding his powers.[46]

---

[44] Safadi, Raed, and Simon Neaime. "Syria: The Painful Transition towards Democracy." Cambridge University Press, Cambridge University Press, 19 Jan. 2017, www.cambridge.org/core/books/abs/democratic-transitions-in-the-arab-world/syria-the-painful-transition-towards-democracy/1A2C9E64199CA7F688C09C 60BB262F67.

[45] Yerkes, Sarah, and Maha Alhomoud. "One Year Later, Tunisia's President Has Reversed Nearly a Decade of Democratic Gains." Carnegieendowment.org, 22 July 2022, carnegieendowment.org/posts/2022/07/one-year-later-tunisias-president-has-reversed-nearly-a-decade-of-democratic-gains?lang=en.

[46] Gokmenoglu, Birgan. "Politics of Anticipation: Turkey's 2017 Constitutional Referendum and the Local "No" Assemblies in Istanbul." Social Movement Studies, no. 4, 3 Mar. 2022, pp. 1–16, https://doi.org/10.1080/14742837.202 2.2047640.

Venezuela, 1998

Hugo Chávez

Elected in 1998, Chávez implemented sweeping constitutional changes that concentrated power in the executive branch. He undermined opposition and independent institutions, setting the stage for authoritarian rule. His successor, Nicolás Maduro, continued this trajectory, turning Venezuela into a de facto dictatorship.[47]

Zimbabwe, 1987

Robert Mugabe

After becoming Prime Minister in 1980 through elections, Mugabe consolidated power over time, abolishing the Prime Minister role in 1987 to become an executive President. He ruled until 2017, using violence, suppression of opposition, and electoral manipulation to maintain power.[48]

The common theme between regimes is that they started as democratically elected leaders and consolidated power over time. Let us establish that the United States is a developed democracy, which separates it from most of these countries. It would be far more difficult for an elected U.S. official to become a dictator than it was for any of the dictators in the above list. That being said, the themes of the events that happened in the above countries are not absent in the U.S. Of the listed countries, many experienced a sharp turning point that significantly

---

[47] LaReau, Renée. "Lessons from Venezuela's Democratic Collapse: How Opposition Movements Can Defy Autocratic Leaders." Keough School of Global Affairs, 21 Mar. 2025, keough.nd.edu/news-and-events/news/lessons-from-venezuelas-democratic-collapse-how-opposition-movements-can-defy-autocratic-leaders/.

[48] Southall, Roger, et al. "History, Tyranny, and Democracy in Zimbabwe." Africa Spectrum, vol. 51, no. 2, 2016, pp. 117–130. JSTOR, www.jstor.org/stable/44982200, https://doi.org/10.2307/44982200.

worsened democracy and personal freedoms, even turning them right from a democracy to a dictatorship in some cases. This is not what the U.S. is in danger of. It is microdoses of themes from the list that will be the killer of our democracy. From 2017 to 2025, one metric finds that the U.S. has declined from 89% free to 84% free.[49] In this time, there have been three presidencies and two presidents,[50] one from each major political party. Each made mistakes that, little by little, cost their constituents many freedoms.[51] Power consolidation, authoritarianism, and corruption in the U.S. government can happen under the rule of any presidency and any party if its citizens are not careful. As citizens, it is our responsibility to pay attention and to keep the flame burning.

---

[49] Freedom House. "United States: Freedom in the World 2025 Country Report | Freedom House." Freedom House, 2025, freedomhouse.org/country/united-states/freedom-world/2025.

[50] Donald J. Trump(2017-2021); Joseph R. Biden(2021-2025); Donald J. Trump(2025)

[51] Find out more: Howell, Jackie. "Trump's Legacy: The Worst President in History & a Lifetime of Failure - Democracy 21." Democracy 21, 13 Mar. 2025, democracy21.org/news/freds-weekly-note/the-worst-president-in-history-a-lifetime-of-failure.
"Hearing Wrap Up: Biden-Harris Administration's Disastrous Record Hurting Americans - United States House Committee on Oversight and Accountability." United States House Committee on Oversight and Accountability, 19 Sept. 2024, oversight.house.gov/release/hearing-wrap-up-biden-harris-administrations-disastrous-record-hurting-americans/.

LOCAL CAMPAIGNS

I try to preserve democracy in the U.S. because I love this country, not because I hate it. The problem is, it can seem really daunting to try to "make change" in such a big country. If you ever feel like it is impossible to make a difference somewhere, make a difference to the next best thing. If you feel like you cannot change the outcome of an election at the national level, try to make change at the state level. If you cannot make change there, start at the local level. I started working on my first campaign when I was sixteen years old and a sophomore in high school. The campaign was for a school board position in my school district, and I was able to work closely with the candidate himself because the campaign team was so small. I realized that as a sixteen-year-old, I was probably not going to change who the president was or the actions of members of the federal government. So, I worked toward making my community more democratic. In this case, the candidate reached out to me and offered that I be on the campaign team. However, most candidates would never think to reach out to community members whom they do not know, especially high school students. I encourage you to connect with candidates yourself and ask them what you can do for the campaign. Attend forums if your town has them, and decide which candidate you like the best, and then reach out. I could not even vote when I was working this campaign, yet, I likely made more of a difference in the outcome of this election than any individual vote would have. And you can too.

During my time working with this campaign, I was able to gain incredible insight as to what happens in campaigns and elections. It should be noted that since this particular campaign was for a school board election, there was no primary election, so most of my work did not start until September of that year, 2023. The campaign started off very normal, entirely what I was expecting it to be like. I will warn you though, working on your first campaign can get shocking toward voting day, because tensions often run high and candidates will personally attack each other. Be prepared for that and do not take it personally. This type of thing happens in almost every election, no matter how small.

I started with the juniors and seniors at my own high school. I made sure that I got others to vote for me(I mean this figuratively; I did not commit voter fraud). Instead, I made sure that the upperclassmen at my school were registered to vote. In the weeks leading up to the election, my friend and I would often come to school early and set up a table in the main hallway. We had a single piece of paper with a QR code on it that took people to an online form required for voter registration. This QR code is easy to find online for every state.[52] In all, we registered over twenty students at our school to vote. It may not seem like much, but in a small town like ours, twenty votes could be enough to determine the outcome of a school board election. When registering people, we did not speak in favor or against any particular candidate, however. I was and still am a firm believer that by simply increasing the amount of people that vote, genuinity and democracy will start to thrive more and more. In other words, while there was no guarantee that the people we registered would vote for the candidate that I was supporting, I was confident in the work of the campaign team and myself, and I was also confident in young people's ability to research and pick a good candidate for our school system.

Then, I wrote letters to the editor in the newspaper in support of the candidate. It was my small town's local newspaper, and it does not have a big audience. But that was no problem, it was enough to promote the candidate, and it was enough to add even the slightest bit of fuel to the flame of democracy.

The trust that I had put in my community and in the eighteen year-olds at my school had paid off. The candidate that I was supporting, the one who I was confident would uplift my community and maximize the quality of education for every single student in the district, had won in

[52] https://autonix.io/qrcodes/voter-registration

a landslide victory. It does not always work out like this, and even if it does not, supporting a candidate's campaign makes that election more competitive. Competitive elections are an integral part of democracy because it not only gives the electorate a variety of options, but it can also make candidates strive to be better in order to be able to win. So, getting involved with a campaign you believe in no matter what level it is will help preserve democracy, regardless of whether or not the candidate wins.

STATE CAMPAIGNS

I was also sixteen years old when I started working on my first state campaign. The candidate that I was helping was running for state representative, meaning she was running for the Ohio House of Representatives. In Ohio alone, there are ninety-nine House districts and thirty-three Senate districts.[53] Together, the state House and the state Senate make up the Ohio General Assembly. Each state has a state House and a state Senate. This operates similar to the national Congress, except that generally there are many more districts and representatives, and decisions made and bills passed affect only the state, not the whole country. Since there are so many districts, especially for the state House, it is not difficult to reach out to candidates and ask what you can do for their campaign. If you are interested in getting involved on state level campaigns, reach out to candidates before the primary election. These are typically either in May or March of the election year, and the general election will be in November. I started helping this particular campaign in September the year before the election, meaning I, and many other volunteers, were working on it for over a year. This was different from the local campaign I had worked on, which was only around two months.

State House and Senate elections operate on the same timeline that national elections do, with House terms being two years and Senate terms being six years.[54] This means that state House elections especially are being planned for constantly, so it is relatively easy to get involved.

---

[53] "Ohio Redistricting Commission." Www.redistricting.ohio.gov, www.redistricting.ohio.gov/.

[54] U.S. House of Representatives. "The House Explained." House.gov, 2017, www.house.gov/the-house-explained.

Candidates will typically start launching their campaigns a few months before the primary election, which is a great opportunity to review their ideas and see which campaign you may want to get involved with. Candidates will likely live near you and maybe even be a part of your community, given the relatively small size of the districts.

Running for state office always improves the democracy in this country, whether or not the candidate wins. There are a couple reasons for this. First, the candidate that won the election will be more likely to think twice about voting for a harmful policy because they will realize that their seat is not guaranteed, especially if the race was close. Running against someone in an election, particularly a powerful incumbent, sets a precedent of standing up to people you believe are inadequate policy-makers.

Second, it can act as a trail-blazing mechanism and pave the way for people that align with your vision of democracy to have a better chance of winning, because of the awareness raised about your agenda and party platform during the campaign. Third, campaigns can bring together people who support democracy and share your political views, and work to educate them more about the processes of campaigns and democracy, so that they can support other related issues in the future. Fourth, campaigns drastically increase civic engagement, which fosters democracy. Campaigns at the state level are generally smaller and give anyone who is interested a chance to help out. A robust democracy features maximum participation from everyone across all groups and sectors of society. Fifth, general awareness can be raised about the shortcomings of current policies that undermine democracy. Campaigns promote education regarding current events and policies, and provide valuable information to the electorate so that they can make the best decisions possible for their communities. So, get involved with a state campaign that you believe in, because win or lose, it can and will make a difference.

ELECTION DAYS

I have been working at the polls during every single election since I have been old enough. If you typically work long hours, then this should be a normal day for you. If not, then be prepared to have a particularly lengthy day. In my home state, Ohio, the polls open at 6:30 AM and close at 7:30 PM. In some states, it is even longer. Further, poll workers are required to arrive at the location at 5:45 AM to help set up, and cannot leave until 8:15 PM because they must help close down. That is fourteen and a half hours that poll workers are legally required to be there, and thirteen hours that they are legally required to be helping voters. It can be an exhausting feat, but I love it more every single election. Due to the fact that all U.S. states legally require locations to be open for a certain number of hours, you might be thinking that it does not matter who volunteers to be a poll worker, and that the polls will still operate the same way. The human capital of being a poll worker is not the main point of volunteering, and that the primary reason that people should sign up to be a poll worker is actually far, far more important.

Estimates show more than one-third of Americans think that the 2020 election was rigged in Biden's favor.[55] If you are walking down the street in an average American town and you see just three people, statistically one of them believes that the 2020 election was rigged. Overall, this demonstrates an extreme distrust in government elections in the U.S. Moreover, there are many ongoing instances of American citizens lacking trust in the government. The Area 51 "raid" in 2019

---

[55] Pengelly, Martin. "More than a Third of US Adults Say Biden's 2020 Victory Was Not Legitimate." The Guardian, 2 Jan. 2024, www.theguardian.com/us-news/2024/jan/02/poll-biden-2020-election-illegitimate.

to see what the government was hiding, the storming of the Capitol Building on January 6th of 2021 after Trump lost the election, and, in general, the copious amounts of people that do not believe in science and believe that it is a government ploy to control its citizens, are all examples of distrust in the American government and its elections. Before the 2024 presidential election, only 37% of Americans believed that the election would be open and honest, with the rest reporting at least some skepticism.[56]

A common theme with all of these examples is that they pose a threat to the stability of American democracy. While people from both parties can admit that gerrymandering, the act of dividing voting districts in a certain group's favor, is a huge problem with the U.S. voting system, the elections are not 'rigged'. While it is true that certain demographics participate in civic engagement more than others, and that there is a high, positive correlation between wealth and civic engagement,[57] the elections are not 'rigged' in the way that some Americans believe. There is no one that is discarding certain votes, or counting one vote multiple times. I have been in the room where voting is taking place and where civilian volunteers are responsible for reporting all votes to the local board of elections, so they can report it to the state, so they can report it to the electoral college, so they can decide where to put their votes, so the country can choose its next president. This process is so secure that it would basically be impossible to rig an election. Digital ballots are stored on computers that are not connected to the internet(meaning a physical device would be required to hack them, which poll workers would quickly notice), and manual ballots are placed in sealed, clear folders and put on tables that anyone walking by can see, which makes it impossible to tamper with or destroy. With each level up the ballots go, the more secure they get. Another misconception is that making

---

[56] Public Affairs Council. "Few Americans Believe 2024 Elections Will Be "Honest and Open."" Public Affairs Council, 12 Mar. 2024, pac.org/impact/few-americans-believe-2024-elections-will-be-honest-and-open.

[57] Garon, Thea, and Christina Plerhoples Stacy. "Civic Engagement Is Higher among Americans Who Are Financially Secure." Urban Institute, 28 Oct. 2024, www.urban.org/urban-wire/civic-engagement-higher-among-americans-who-are-financially-secure.

a mistake on a ballot can disqualify the vote. In reality, you will be notified by a poll worker if your ballot contains a mistake or ambiguity so that you can fix it. Nonetheless, the notion that U.S. elections are literally rigged in this way poses a direct threat to our democracy, which can be concretely seen from the Capitol insurrections, and refusal of a peaceful transition of power by Donald Trump after the 2020 election.[58]

When I work at the polls, part of my job is to give voters two options to vote. The first is the one that almost everyone chooses, the digital ballot. The digital ballot is easy; you can change your text size and brightness, and there is even a read aloud option for those that are hard of hearing. Besides that, the digital ballot is now considered the "normal" way to vote. We, the poll workers, simply scan the voter's ID and send them on their way to the computer box. The second option, however, is the manual ballot. With the manual ballot, it is a bit of an ordeal. We have to first get the voter's ID number, then tear out a piece of paper that matches the subdivision. Next, we tear off a piece of paper at the top, and sort them into plastic bags in order to manually report them to the local board of elections at the end of the day. Additionally, we can only hope it is not the primary election, because then we also have to select the democrat, republican, or issues only paper. This can create some tension, as many people, understandably in the current political climate, do not want to say their party affiliation aloud.

Despite the increased hassle that the manual ballot creates, I have concluded that one of the most important parts of being a poll worker is acting completely normal when a voter requests a manual ballot, as if it is not a slight inconvenience. I often describe both options, digital and manual, to voters because some people get the two confused, and want the digital ballot in reality. However, it is crucial not to convince them to select the manual ballot.

This brings me to my main point. The reason that people should volunteer to work at the polls on election days is not because the polls need the human capital, in most places anyway, but because it allows people to trust the election system more. The reason that people select

58 Crowley, Michael. "Trump Won't Commit to "Peaceful" Post-Election Transfer of Power." The New York Times, 24 Sept. 2020, www.nytimes. com/2020/09/23/us/politics/trump-power-transfer-2020-election.html.

the manual ballot could be that it is what they are used to. However, an allegedly much more common reason is that they do not trust the digital ballots to be counted properly. I understand why people are suspicious of elections. There is so much yellow journalism on the internet claiming that elections are rigged, and this comes from both parties. More people working at polls works to protect democracy in the United States in this regard. People are less likely to have distrust in people that are similar to them, such as the people in their community(voting is regional). People we see often are far easier to trust than people in high levels of the government, because people in close proximity are more relatable and similar to us.[59] So, people volunteering to work at the polls actively preserve democracy. Acting normally when someone selects the manual ballot and volunteering at the polls in general, go a long way to protect democracy. You can usually sign up by emailing the board of elections for your county and letting them know that you are interested in becoming a poll worker. If you are at all able, please get out and help at the polls just twice a year.

[59] Clerke, Alexa S., and Erin A. Heerey. "The Influence of Similarity and Mimicry on Decisions to Trust." Collabra: Psychology, vol. 7, no. 1, 2021, https://doi.org/10.1525/collabra.23441.

DANGERS OF BOTH EXTREMES
OF AUTHORITARIANISM

In 2025, it is socially unacceptable almost everywhere in the U.S. to want the country to become fascist, with the term commonly being used as an insult.[60] Fascism has been responsible for the demise of many individuals, and oftentimes entire people groups. The most infamous example of fascism is the Nazi regime that occurred in Germany and spread across Europe in the 1930s and 1940s.[61] Characteristics of facism, by definition and example, include violence and discrimination, extreme nationalism, manipulative propaganda, and overreaching militarization. In fact, more than ninety percent of the American electorate views these things as evil and believes that fascism should not be implemented in any government.[62]

Conversely, communism is far more acceptable. The Red Scare occurred in the United States in the 1910s, and then again in the 1940s and 1950s.[63] However, overtime, perhaps because the Soviet Union

---

[60] Daniels, Mitch. "Opinion | Tossing around "Nazi" and "Fascist" as Insults Is Reckless and Historically Illiterate." Washington Post, 19 July 2021, www.washingtonpost.com/opinions/2021/07/11/tossing-around-nazi-fascist-insults-is-reckless-historically-illitcrate/.

[61] Britannica. "Nazi Party | Definition, Meaning, History, & Facts." Encyclopædia Britannica, 26 Sept. 2018, www.britannica.com/topic/Nazi-Party.

[62] "Share of Americans Who Believe It's Acceptable to Hold Neo-Nazi/White Supremacist Views, August 2017." Statista, Aug. 2017, www.statista.com/statistics/740001/share-of-americans-who-think-neo-nazi-views-are-acceptable-to-have/.

[63] Miller Center. "McCarthyism and the Red Scare." Miller Center, University of Virginia, 2025, millercenter.org/the-presidency/educational-resources/age-of-eisenhower/mcarthyism-red-scare.

dissolved, claiming to support communism, especially online, has become relatively common and accepted, at least among my generation.[64] That is not to say that it is socially acceptable, it is just more acceptable than fascism. If you claim to be a communist, some people will be upset, some will disagree strongly, and some will think that you are insane. However, given the choice between publicly claiming to be a communist and publicly claiming to be a fascist, most people would choose the former, because it is largely more socially acceptable, with almost half of the electorate viewing it favorably.[65] Let us examine every communist regime in history in order to think about communism and what role it might play in the United States. Note that this is a short history, as communism was not formally implemented until the twentieth century, and there have only ever been twenty-six confirmed regimes.

---

[64] Clemens, Jason. "Young Americans Support Abstract and Unworkable Socialism." Fraser Institute, 2023, www.fraserinstitute.org/commentary/young-americans-support-abstract-and-unworkable-socialism. Accessed 3 June 2025.

[65] Montgomery, David. "Would Americans Choose Communism or Fascism?" Yougov.com, YouGov, 18 Oct. 2024, today.yougov.com/politics/articles/50737-would-americans-choose-communism-or-fascism.

COMMUNISM

Afghanistan, 1978

The communist regime began after the Saur Revolution, when the People's Democratic Party of Afghanistan (PDPA) seized power. The regime implemented radical reforms, including land redistribution and secularization, which provoked widespread unrest, especially among rural and religious groups. This led to a brutal civil conflict and prompted the Soviet Union to invade in 1979 to support the PDPA. The conflict and repression under the regime and during the war caused widespread devastation, with an estimated total death toll of around two million people.[66]

Albania, 1946

Albania's communist regime started under Enver Hoxha, following World War II. The country became one of the most isolated and repressive communist states in the world. Hoxha implemented strict Stalinist policies, abolished religion, and established a secret police force to crush dissent. During this period, widespread purges, executions, and harsh imprisonment contributed to a death toll estimated around twenty thousand people, over six thousand of which were executions.[67]

---

[66] Weinbaum, Marvin G., and Nancy Hatch Durpee. "Afghanistan - Civil War, Communist Phase (1978–92)." Encyclopedia Britannica, www.britannica.com/place/Afghanistan/Civil-war-communist-phase-1978-92.

[67] Ypi, Lea. "Albania's History of Communism and Postcommunism Has a Message for Our Time." Jacobin.com, 26 July 2022, jacobin.com/2022/07/albania-history-communism-postcommunism-hoxha-liberalism.

Angola, 1975

Angola's communist regime emerged after it gained independence from Portugal. The Marxist-Leninist People's Movement for the Liberation of Angola (MPLA) took power, leading to a brutal civil war against rival factions. The MPLA, backed by the Soviet Union and Cuba, established a one-party socialist state and maintained control through military force, nationalization, and political repression.[68] The civil war lasted until 2002. The conflict and associated repression under the communist regime contributed to a death toll estimated at six hundred thousand people.

Benin, 1975

Benin, formerly known as Dahomey, became a Marxist-Leninist state under Major Mathieu Kérékou. The regime adopted socialist policies such as nationalization of industries, centralized planning, and alignment with the Soviet bloc. Political opposition was suppressed, and dissenters were often imprisoned or executed. The estimated death toll from political repression during Benin's communist era is relatively low, likely around two hundred.[69]

Bulgaria, 1946

Bulgaria became a communist state under the leadership of the Bulgarian Communist Party and strong influence from the Soviet Union. Todor Zhivkov ruled the country from 1954 to 1989, overseeing a tightly controlled one-party state. The regime carried out political purges, suppressed dissent, and operated a network of secret police. Notably, it also attempted forced assimilation of ethnic minorities, particularly the Turkish population, through the "Revival Process." The estimated

---

[68] The Editors of Encyclopaedia Britannica. "Angola - Independence and Civil War | Britannica." Encyclopædia Britannica, 2019, www.britannica.com/place/Angola/Independence-and-civil-war.

[69] ProleWiki. "People's Republic of Benin (1975–1990) - ProleWiki." ProleWiki, 4 Nov. 2024, en.prolewiki.org/wiki/People%27s_Republic_of_Benin_(1975%E2%80%931990).

death toll from executions, labor camps, and political repression during Bulgaria's communist period is around <u>twenty-five thousand</u>.[70]

Cambodia, 1975

Cambodia's communist regime, led by the Khmer Rouge under Pol Pot, ruled from 1975 to 1979 and was one of the most brutal in history. After seizing power, the regime sought to create a classless, agrarian society by abolishing money, private property, religion, and urban life. Intellectuals, professionals, ethnic minorities, and anyone suspected of disloyalty were targeted. Mass executions, forced labor, starvation, and disease annihilated the population. During its short rule, the Khmer Rouge was responsible for the deaths of approximately <u>two million</u> people, about a quarter of Cambodia's population.[71]

China, 1949

China's communist regime started when the Chinese Communist Party, led by Mao Zedong, established the People's Republic of China. The early decades were marked by sweeping campaigns to reshape society, including land reforms, the Great Leap Forward (1958–1962), and the Cultural Revolution (1966–1976). These efforts aimed to eliminate class enemies and enforce strict communist ideology but resulted in widespread chaos, famine, and political persecution. The Great Leap Forward alone caused an estimated thirty to forty-five million deaths due to starvation and forced labor, while the Cultural Revolution led to the deaths and persecution of millions more. Overall, the estimated death toll under Mao's rule is <u>seventy million</u> people, making it one of

---

[70] Dimitrov, Phillip, and Loring Danforth. "Bulgaria - the Early Communist Era." Encyclopedia Britannica, www.britannica.com/place/Bulgaria/The-early-communist-era.

[71] United States Holocaust memorial museum. "Origins of the Khmer Rouge - United States Holocaust Memorial Museum." Www.ushmm.org, 2024, www.ushmm.org/genocide-prevention/countries/cambodia/origins-of-the-khmer-rouge.

the deadliest regimes in history. China is currently still a communist country in 2025.[72]

Cuba, 1959

Cuba's communist regime began after Fidel Castro overthrew the U.S.-backed Batista dictatorship. The new government aligned with the Soviet Union and implemented sweeping socialist reforms, including land redistribution, nationalization of industries, and suppression of political opposition. Over time, Cuba became a one-party state under the Communist Party, with tight control over media, expression, and civil liberties. Political dissenters were imprisoned, exiled, or executed, especially in the early decades. While Cuba did not experience the mass death tolls seen in some other communist regimes, estimates suggest that thousands to tens of thousands died due to political executions, imprisonment, and escape attempts. Commonly cited figures estimate around <u>ten thousand</u> deaths. Cuba is currently still a communist country in 2025.[73]

Czechoslovakia, 1948

Czechoslovakia became a communist state after a Soviet-backed coup brought the Communist Party to power. The regime quickly established a one-party system, suppressed dissent, and nationalized industry. Political trials, imprisonments, and executions followed, especially during the Stalinist period. In 1968, the Prague Spring, an attempt to liberalize the regime, was crushed by a Warsaw Pact invasion, leading to a period of repression known as "Normalization." While less deadly than in some other Eastern Bloc countries, political persecution was significant. The estimated death toll due to executions, forced labor, and prison conditions under Czechoslovakia's communist regime is around

---

[72] The Investopedia Team. "Great Leap Forward." Investopedia, 16 Sept. 2022, www.investopedia.com/terms/g/great-leap-forward.asp.

[73] The Editors of the Encyclopedia Britannica. "Communist Party of Cuba | Political Party, Cuba." Encyclopædia Britannica, 20 Dec. 2018, www.britannica.com/topic/Communist-Party-of-Cuba.

four thousand people. Note that Czechoslovakia no longer exists as a sovereign nation.[74]

East Germany, 1949

East Germany, officially the German Democratic Republic (GDR), was established as a Soviet-aligned communist state. Governed by the Socialist Unity Party (SED), it maintained strict control over all aspects of life through surveillance, censorship, and repression, primarily enforced by the Stasi. Political dissent was harshly punished, and attempts to flee to West Germany were met with deadly force, especially at the Berlin Wall. While the regime did not carry out mass purges on the scale of the Soviet Union, it was responsible for an estimated <u>one thousand</u> deaths from border killings and thousands more imprisoned or persecuted for political reasons. Note that East Germany no longer exists as a sovereign nation.[75]

Ethiopia, 1974

Ethiopia's communist regime, known as the Derg, came to power after overthrowing Emperor Haile Selassie. Led by Mengistu Haile Mariam, the Marxist-Leninist government nationalized land and industries and launched a campaign called the "Red Terror" to eliminate opposition. Thousands of suspected dissidents were executed, tortured, or imprisoned. The regime also faced multiple armed rebellions and famines amplified by its policies. The estimated death toll from political repression, executions, famine, and conflict during the Derg's rule is around <u>one million</u> people.[76]

---

[74] Dana. "Communism in Czechoslovakia: How It All Started and Ended | Prague behind the Scenes." Prague behind the Scenes, 18 Aug. 2022, www.praguebehindthescenes.com/communism-in-czechoslovakia/.

[75] Strauss, Gerald, and George Hall Kirby. "Germany - the East German System." Encyclopedia Britannica, www.britannica.com/place/Germany/The-East-German-system.

[76] Parker, Ben. "UNDP EMERGENCIES UNIT for ETHIOPIA." Www.africa.upenn.edu, www.africa.upenn.edu/eue_web/redterr.htm.

Grenada, 1979

Grenada's communist-influenced regime began when the Marxist-Leninist New Jewel Movement, led by Maurice Bishop, overthrew the government in a coup. The regime aimed to implement socialist reforms and aligned itself with Cuba and the Soviet Union. The regime was short-lived and marked by political violence, but the overall death toll was relatively low, estimated at around <u>one hundred</u> people.[77]

Hungary, 1949

Hungary became a communist state after World War II. The Hungarian Working People's Party established a one-party regime that suppressed political opposition, controlled the economy, and enforced strict social conformity. In 1956, a nationwide uprising known as the Hungarian Revolution challenged Soviet control but was violently crushed by Soviet forces, resulting in thousands of deaths. Throughout the communist period, political repression, show trials, and imprisonment were common. The estimated death toll from executions, political violence, and repression during Hungary's communist era is around <u>five thousand</u> people.[78] Laos became a communist state when the Pathet Lao, backed by North Vietnam and the Soviet Union, took control after years of civil war. The new Lao People's Democratic Republic established a one-party socialist government, implementing collectivization and strict political control. The regime suppressed opposition, leading to imprisonment, forced relocations, and executions, especially targeting ethnic minorities and former royalists. While exact numbers are difficult to determine, estimates suggest that the death toll related to political repression, purges, and war during the communist takeover and early rule is around

---

[77] Sunkara, Bhaskar. "The US Invaded the Island of Grenada 40 Years Ago. The Legacy of Revolution Lives On." The Guardian, 25 Oct. 2023, www.theguardian.com/commentisfree/2023/oct/25/the-us-invaded-the-island-of-grenada-40-years-ago-the-legacy-of-revolution-lives-on.

[78] Vardy, Steven Bela. "History of Hungary - Hungary in the Soviet Orbit | Britannica." Www.britannica.com, www.britannica.com/topic/history-of-Hungary/Hungary-in-the-Soviet-orbit.

sixty thousand people. Laos is currently still a communist country in 2025.[79]

Mongolia, 1924

Mongolia became a communist state under influence from the Soviet Union, establishing the Mongolian People's Republic. The communist regime implemented communist policies, including collectivization and suppression of religion and traditional culture. During the 1930s, under leader Khorloogiin Choibalsan, the government carried out brutal purges targeting political opponents, intellectuals, religious leaders, and ethnic minorities. Thousands were executed or sent to labor camps. Estimates of the death toll during Mongolia's communist purges and repression indicate a total of thirty thousand deaths.[80]

Mozambique, 1975

Mozambique's communist regime began when the Marxist-Leninist party FRELIMO took power after independence from Portugal. The new government nationalized land and industries and sought to transform society through socialist policies. However, the regime faced a brutal civil war against the anti-communist insurgent group RENAMO, backed by Rhodesia and South Africa. This conflict, combined with political repression and economic hardship, caused widespread suffering. The estimated total death toll from the communist regime's policies, the civil war, and related violence is around one million people.[81]

---

[79] BBC. "Laos Country Profile." BBC News, 18 Apr. 2023, www.bbc.com/news/world-asia-pacific-15351898.

[80] Chapple, Amoc "Mongolia, the Forgotten Soviet Satellite." RadioFreeEurope/RadioLiberty, RFE/RL, 15 Oct. 2024, www.rferl.org/a/mongolia-soviet-era-photos-communism-socialism-democracy/33155566.html.

[81] Munslow, Barry. "Mozambique: Marxism-Leninism in Reverse, the Fifth Congress of Frelimo." Journal of Communist Studies, vol. 6, no. 1, Mar. 1990, pp. 109–112, https://doi.org/10.1080/13523279008415011. Accessed 21 Jan. 2021.

North Korea, 1948

North Korea's communist regime was established under Kim Il-sung. The regime is characterized by a totalitarian dictatorship, extreme isolation, and a cult of personality around the Kim family. It has maintained strict control through a pervasive security apparatus, political purges, forced labor camps, and severe restrictions on freedoms. The government's policies, combined with famine in the 1990s and ongoing human rights abuses, have caused immense suffering. Estimates of the total death toll from political repression, famines, and labor camps under the North Korean regime range widely but are generally around two million people. There is debate about whether or not North Korea is a communist country in 2025.[82]

North Vietnam, 1945

North Vietnam was a communist state established under Ho Chi Minh's leadership. North Vietnam implemented socialist reforms, land redistribution, and strict political control over its population. The war caused immense destruction and loss of life, including civilian casualties from bombings, fighting, and political repression. While it's difficult to separate deaths caused directly by the regime from those caused by the war, estimates suggest that the total death toll related to North Vietnam's communist rule and the conflict is around one and a half million people, including military and civilian deaths. Note that North Vietnam no longer exists as a sovereign nation.[83]

Poland, 1947

Poland became a communist state after World War II. Officially known as the Polish People's Republic, the regime was controlled by the Polish United Workers' Party and closely aligned with the USSR. It suppressed

---

[82] "North Korea Country Profile." BBC News, 13 June 2018, www.bbc.com/news/world-asia-pacific-15256929.

[83] Spector, Ronald H. "Vietnam War." Britannica, 14 Nov. 2018, www.britannica.com/event/Vietnam-War.

political opposition, censored the media, and used secret police to maintain control. Key flashpoints included the Stalinist purges of the late 1940s and early 1950s, the violent quelling of protests in 1956 and 1970, and the imposition of martial law in 1981 to crush the Solidarity movement. The estimated death toll from executions, prison conditions, and violent crackdowns is around <u>twenty thousand</u> people.[84]

Republic of the Congo, 1969

The Republic of the Congo (Congo-Brazzaville) became a Marxist-Leninist state under President Marien Ngouabi, who established the Congolese Party of Labour (PCT) as the sole ruling party. The regime aligned closely with the Soviet Union and Cuba, nationalized industries, and implemented socialist policies. Political repression, purges, and internal power struggles were frequent. Subsequent leaders continued the one-party rule until the early 1990s. While the regime was authoritarian, it was not among the most violent communist states. The estimated death toll from political purges, repression, and related violence during the communist period is around <u>three thousand</u> people.[85]

Romania, 1947

Romania's communist regime began when the monarchy was abolished and the Romanian Communist Party took power. Under Gheorghe Gheorghiu-Dej and later Nicolae Ceaușescu, Romania became a highly repressive police state. Ceaușescu's rule (1965–1989) was marked by a brutal secret police (Securitate), widespread surveillance, severe censorship, forced relocations, and disastrous economic policies, including extreme austerity that led to mass poverty and malnutrition. Political dissent was harshly punished through imprisonment, torture, and execution. The regime collapsed violently in 1989 during the

---

[84] "Research Guides: Polish-American Relations, 1918 to Present: Manuscript Resources at the Library of Congress: Polish People's Republic. Poland under Communism (1946-1989)." Loc.gov, 2015, guides.loc.gov/poland-manuscripts/collections3.

[85] "The Congo, Decolonization, and the Cold War, 1960–1965." Office of the Historian, history.state.gov/milestones/1961-1968/congo-decolonization.

Romanian Revolution. The estimated death toll under Romania's communist regime is <u>eighty</u> <u>thousand</u> people, including victims of repression, labor camps, and the 1989 uprising.[86]

Somalia, 1969

Somalia's communist regime rose when General Siad Barre seized power in a coup and established the Somali Democratic Republic. Barre adopted a Marxist-Leninist ideology, aligning closely with the Soviet Union and later China. His regime implemented socialist policies such as land nationalization and secularization, while suppressing clan-based opposition through brutal crackdowns. In the late 1970s, after a failed war with Ethiopia over the Ogaden region, the regime lost Soviet support and became increasingly authoritarian and violent. Repression, torture, and massacres, particularly against the Isaaq clan, were widespread. The estimated death toll from Barre's regime, including political repression and civil conflict, is around <u>seventy thousand</u> people, with tens of thousands killed during the Isaaq genocide alone.[87]

South Yemen, 1967

South Yemen, officially the People's Democratic Republic of Yemen, became a Marxist-Leninist state after gaining independence from British colonial rule. The regime implemented radical land reforms, nationalized industries, and repressed tribal and religious structures. It was marked by political purges, internal party violence, and crackdowns on dissent. The estimated total death toll from political purges, repression, and conflict during South Yemen's communist period is <u>ten</u>

---

[86] Hitchens, Keith Arnold. "Romania - Communist Romania | Britannica." Encyclopædia Britannica, 2020,_ www.britannica.com/place/Romania/Communist-Romania.

[87] Office of the Historian. "Milestones: 1977–1980 - Office of the Historian." History.state.gov, history.state.gov/milestones/1977-1980/horn-of-africa.

<u>thousand</u> people. Note that South Yemen no longer exists as a sovereign nation.[88]

Soviet Union(USSR), 1922

The Soviet Union, founded after the Russian Revolution, was the first and most influential communist state, led initially by Vladimir Lenin and then by Joseph Stalin and subsequent leaders. Under Stalin (1924–1953), the regime carried out mass purges, forced collectivization, widespread executions, and the creation of a vast system of labor camps (Gulags). Millions died from political repression, man-made famines (such as the Holodomor in Ukraine, which was a part of the Soviet Union), and harsh labor conditions. Repression continued under later leaders, though with less intensity. Estimates of the total death toll under the Soviet communist regime vary widely but generally is around <u>twenty-five million</u> people, with some estimates far higher, depending on how war-related and famine deaths are counted.[89]

Vietnam, 1975

Vietnam became a unified communist state after North Vietnam defeated South Vietnam and the U.S.-backed government collapsed. The ruling Communist Party imposed Marxist-Leninist policies across the country, including land collectivization, re-education camps for former South Vietnamese officials and intellectuals, and restrictions on political and religious freedoms. Hundreds of thousands were sent to labor camps, and many died due to harsh conditions. Additionally, a mass exodus of "boat people" fleeing persecution led to many deaths at sea. The estimated death toll from executions, re-education camps, and

---

[88] Ishiyama, John. "Communism and Organizational Symbiosis in South Yemen." Communist Parties in the Middle East, 17 May 2019, pp. 168–183, https://doi.org/10.4324/9780367134464-9.

[89] "Soviet Union Timeline." BBC News, 31 Oct. 2013, www.bbc.com/news/world-europe-17858981.

the refugee crisis is around <u>three hundred thousand</u> people. Vietnam is currently still a communist country in 2025.[90]

Yugoslavia, 1945

Yugoslavia became a communist state after World War II under Josip Broz Tito, who led the Partisans to victory and established the Socialist Federal Republic of Yugoslavia. Though communist, Tito broke from Stalin in 1948 and pursued a more independent and decentralized form of socialism known as "Titoism." The regime suppressed political dissent, especially in its early years, with secret police, political prisons, and executions. Ethnic tensions were tightly controlled under Tito's rule but flared violently after the state's collapse in the 1990s. Estimates of deaths due to political purges, repression, and forced labor during the communist era is around <u>one hundred fifty thousand</u> people. Note that Yugoslavia no longer exists as a sovereign nation.[91]

So, back to the question, why do some supporters of human rights also support communism? The sum of the underlined numbers from each regime is 105,888,300. This is a rough estimate, and each underlined figure is an approximation based on numbers from various sources. Regardless, that is over one hundred million people that died, in most cases quite brutally, because of communism. Note also that all but four(arguably five) of these regimes fell. This list includes every single communist regime in history in which the state was fully communist, not just one party. Every single one of these regimes included brutal violence perpetrated by the government and a nonzero death toll. Of the regimes that have not failed yet, gross human rights abuses are happening. No country's government is perfect and there is no country that does not have any human rights abuses, at least to some degree, but

90 Young, Jin Yu, and Sui-Lee Wee. "Here's What to Know about Vietnam's Communist Government." The New York Times, 20 Mar. 2024, www.nytimes.com/2024/03/20/world/asia/vietnam-government-communism.html.
91 Allcock, John B., and John R. Lampe. "Yugoslavia | History, Map, Breakup, & Facts." Encyclopædia Britannica, 16 Nov. 2018, www.britannica.com/place/Yugoslavia-former-federated-nation-1929-2003.

China,[92] Cuba,[93] Laos,[94] North Korea,[95] and Vietnam[96] are among the worst in the world. This means that there has never been a successful communist regime, with no casualties, that did not have grave human rights abuses. Twenty-six countries have ever been fully communist, and not a single one accomplished what communism supporters think it will accomplish: classlessness, peace, and equality.

If you were unhappy at your current job, and you were unable to find a better one, would you stay at your current job until you could find a better one, or would you switch to a worse one in the meantime? What about if you lived in an unsafe neighborhood? Would you move to one with an even higher crime rate if you could not find a safer one, or would you stick with your current one until you could? Capitalism and the current way the U.S. government runs is frustrating for most people. It is difficult for many to find a good job, pay loans, and afford a house among other necessities. Capitalism is not a good system. However, it is the best, or rather least bad, system humans have invented thus far. To make the U.S. more democratic and increase the quality of life for Americans, we should be in search of a new system.

There are some limitations to this trend, however. The idea of communism is relatively young, as it started in the early 1900s with Soviet Russia. Due to this, there is an argument to be made that its age is the reason for its lack of success thus far, and that it has not been given a chance. Additionally, most of the nations that have ever been communist were communist when the USSR was a global power, and it had a large influence on many of these countries. A claim could be

[92] Freedom House. "China: Freedom in the World 2025 Country Report | Freedom House." Freedom House, 2024, freedomhouse.org/country/china/freedom-world/2025.

[93] "Cuba: Freedom in the World 2025 Country Report | Freedom House." Freedom House, 2024, freedomhouse.org/country/cuba/freedom-world/2025.

[94] "Laos: Freedom in the World 2024 Country Report." Freedom House, 2024, freedomhouse.org/country/laos/freedom-world/2024.

[95] "North Korea: Freedom in the World 2024 Country Report." Freedom House, 2024, freedomhouse.org/country/north-korea/freedom-world/2024.

[96] "Vietnam: Freedom in the World 2024 Country Report." Freedom House, 2024, freedomhouse.org/country/vietnam/freedom-world/2024.

made with regards to this that the evils of most of the regimes were a result of Soviet influence, and not due to communism itself.

That being said, any system that has caused over one hundred million deaths among copious amounts of other human rights abuses needs some very close research, thinking, investigating, and changing before anyone should consider supporting it or advertising it as the solution to issues presented by capitalism.

FASCISM

While fascism is not an inherently economic system the way communism and capitalism are, it does have implications for the economy that will be considered below. The most well-known examples of fascist governments are Germany, Italy, and Japan(debatably) during World War II. Clearly, based on these examples alone, most Americans would agree that fascism is an unacceptable form of governing. The most dangerous thing about fascism seems to be when characteristics of it subtly appear in governmental proceedings. It is well known that many Americans, especially Democrats, view Trump as a fascist.[97] Let us examine a few agreed upon characteristics and stages of fascism[98] and how they have appeared in the government in presidencies.[99]

Characteristics

Extreme Nationalism

Fascist regimes favor certain groups of people over others. Patriotism and loyalty to one's country are taken to the extreme and minority groups in the country become heavily discriminated against, sometimes to the

---

[97] Langer, Gary, and Steven Sparks. "Half of Americans See Donald Trump as a Fascist: POLL." ABC News, 25 Oct. 2024, abcnews.go.com/Politics/donald-trump-fascist-concerns-poll/story?id=115083795.

[98] Council on Foreign Relations. "What Is Fascism?" CFR Education from the Council on Foreign Relations, Council on Foreign Relations, 14 Apr. 2023, education.cfr.org/learn/reading/what-fascism.

[99] While I normally include examples of threats from each main political party if applicable, fascism is specifically characteristic of extreme right-wing agendas, so I will include only Trump's presidency.

point of murder. Extreme nationalism is at the heart of fascist ideology. Fascist leaders exploit patriotic sentiment, transforming healthy pride in one's nation into an exclusionary and aggressive force. The nation is portrayed as a sacred entity under attack by foreigners, minority groups, or alleged internal enemies who are accused of weakening its unity. In Mussolini's Italy, this took the form of glorifying the Roman Empire and suppressing ethnic and political minorities. In Nazi Germany, it led to genocidal policies justified by racial purity and national rebirth.

This form of nationalism redefines belonging, and not everyone is seen as a true citizen, only those who conform to a narrow, idealized vision of the nation. Symbols like flags, slogans, and militaristic imagery are used to enforce conformity and demand absolute loyalty. Dissent is labeled as betrayal, and diversity becomes seen as a threat rather than a strength.

In the United States, similar rhetoric sometimes appears when political leaders equate patriotism with obedience or vilify those who protest injustice as un-American. To prevent nationalism from curdling into fascism, it is essential to promote an inclusive form of patriotism: one that celebrates shared democratic values rather than ethnic, racial, or cultural homogeneity. True loyalty to the U.S. means striving to make it live up to its ideals of equality, freedom, and justice for all.

Cult of Personality

A defining feature of fascist movements is the cult of personality: the elevation of a single leader to divine status. Fascist regimes rely on strong, charismatic figures who claim to embody the people and destiny of the nation. These leaders present themselves as infallible and uniquely capable of restoring order and greatness. Mussolini styled himself as "Il Duce," or "The Leader," while Hitler became "Der Führer." Their images appeared in posters, movies, and classrooms, cultivating a loyalty that prioritized blind devotion over critical thinking.

The cult of personality serves a critical function in fascism: it fuses personal loyalty to the leader with loyalty to the state itself. Any criticism of the leader becomes an attack on the nation. Over time, this dynamic erodes democratic institutions, as people come to trust one individual more than the law, the press, or representative government. Rational debate is replaced by emotional spectacle, and the truth becomes whatever the leader says it is.

In the United States, similar tendencies emerge when political figures are treated as saviors rather than public servants. When crowds chant their names, dismiss all criticism as "fake news," or claim that only one person can fix the country. Combating this requires a renewed commitment to democratic principles: valuing institutions over individuals, facts over propaganda, and collective responsibility over worship of politicians. A healthy democracy depends on citizens who question their leaders, not ones who idolize them.

Popular Mobilization

Another hallmark of fascism is popular mobilization: the organized effort to turn enthusiasm into political power. Fascist leaders do not rely solely on traditional institutions; instead, they actively seek to involve ordinary citizens in rallies, marches, and youth organizations. These movements create the illusion of unity and strength, as people chant slogans, wave flags, and pledge loyalty to the regime. In Mussolini's Italy and Hitler's Germany, these performances transformed politics into theater, where emotion had power over reason.

Popular mobilization also serves to intimidate opponents and silence dissent. When people see vast crowds cheering a single leader, they begin to believe resistance is dangerous. Propaganda and mass media amplify this effect, portraying the movement as the unstoppable will of "the people."

Participation becomes a social expectation. People who refuse to join are branded as traitors or enemies.

In the United States, similar dynamics can emerge when political rallies become charged with aggression or when social media turns politics into a contest of loyalty rather than ideas. When citizens are encouraged to follow slogans instead of policies, democracy weakens. To counter this, Americans must channel civic energy into constructive participation, such as voting, volunteering, engaging in community dialogue, and holding leaders accountable. Democratic mobilization empowers individuals to think critically and act independently, rather than lose themselves in a movement.

Stages

The five stages of fascism as written by scholar Robert Paxton explain how fascists in the past have come to power, specifically Mussolini and Hitler.[100] Let us examine similarities with the U.S. and outline what we can do to combat them.

1. Disillusionment

Disillusionment occurs when people are unhappy with the status quo in their country, or they realize that the current state of affairs is not as good as they once believed. One 2025 poll finds that only 38% of Americans are satisfied with the current state of the nation.[101] Disillusionment with the U.S. economy has grown as more people feel that the promise of upward mobility, part of the "American Dream", is slipping out of reach. While corporate profits hit record highs, millions struggle with stagnant wages, rising housing costs, student debt, and limited access to affordable healthcare.[102] The wealth gap is also an issue, and many feel that the system is rigged in favor of the wealthy and well-connected. This sense of economic betrayal is especially strong among younger generations, who often earn less and face higher living costs than their parents did.[103]

[100] Paxton, Robert O. "The Five Stages of Fascism." The Journal of Modern History, vol. 70, no. 1, Mar. 1998, pp. 1–23, www.jstor.org/stable/10.1086/235001.

[101] Saad, Lydia. "Americans' State of the Nation Ratings Remain at Record Low." Gallup.com, Gallup, 5 Feb. 2025, news.gallup.com/poll/656114/americans-state-nation-ratings-remain-record-low.aspx.

[102] Nadeem, Reem. "Americans Continue to View Several Economic Issues as Top National Problems." Pew Research Center, 20 Feb. 2025, www.pewresearch.org/politics/2025/02/20/americans-continue-to-view-several-economic-issues-as-top-national-problems/.

[103] Williams, Austin. "Data Reveals What's More Expensive Now than 1990 – and What's Cheaper." LiveNOW from FOX | Breaking News, Live Events, LiveNOW from FOX, 19 Dec. 2024, www.livenowfox.com/news/price-changes-since-1990.

This widespread disillusionment creates ground for authoritarian and extremist movements. According to Robert Paxton's model, fascism often begins when citizens lose faith in existing institutions and traditional political parties. In both Mussolini's Italy and Hitler's Germany, this despair allowed charismatic leaders to present themselves as saviors who could restore national pride and order. Similarly, in the U.S. today, some politicians exploit public frustration by blaming society's problems on scapegoats: immigrants, minorities, or the media. They claim that only they can fix the system, eroding trust in democratic norms and institutions.

To combat this stage of fascism, the solution lies in addressing the root causes of disillusionment. Strengthening social safety nets, expanding access to affordable housing, healthcare, and education, and ensuring fair wages can help rebuild faith in democracy's ability to deliver for everyone, not just the wealthy few. Civic education, community engagement, and media literacy are equally vital, empowering citizens to recognize manipulation and resist demagogic appeals. When people feel secure, represented, and hopeful about their future, the lure of authoritarian quick fixes loses its power.

2. Legitimacy

This stage is when a fascist leader will create their own political party and establish the legitimacy of it over time. In the beginning, the movement usually starts independent of politics, and is often dismissed as radical and extreme. However, the leader capitalizes on widespread frustration, such as economic hardship, social unrest, or political gridlock. The movement begins to attract attention. The fascist leader presents themselves as a voice for the "common people," offering strong, decisive leadership in contrast to what they frame as the weakness or corruption of existing political institutions.

As the party grows, it starts to build alliances with powerful groups that can help it gain influence. Business elites, traditional conservatives, and even associates of the military may begin to support the fascists, either out of fear of socialism, desire for stability, or belief that they can control the movement for their own ends. These partnerships help the fascist leader gain credibility and resources, further embedding the movement into mainstream politics.

Over time, propaganda and mass mobilization play a significant role in normalizing the party's presence. The leader uses speeches, rallies, and media campaigns to shape public opinion, portraying the party as the only force capable of saving the nation. Eventually, through legal means, such as elections, coalitions, or appointments, the fascist movement secures real political power. At this point, what began as a fringe ideology becomes a legitimate force in government, setting the stage for the next phase: the consolidation of absolute control. Some political trends in recent years display elements of this stage.

The rise of extremist groups, the use of misinformation to discredit democratic institutions, and the framing of opponents as "enemies of the nation" reflect tactics that have historically helped authoritarian movements gain legitimacy. These parallels are warnings of how fragile democracy can be when fear and division are used as political tools.

3. Right-Wing Partnerships

This stage is when the fascist movement begins forming strategic alliances with right-wing or conservative groups to gain political power. At this point, the movement is still not strong enough to take control on its own, so it seeks legitimacy and influence by partnering with established political figures, wealthy elites, or traditional institutions like the military and the church. These groups often see the fascists as useful allies who can suppress left-wing movements, restore social order, and protect their economic interests.

The partnership is usually built on shared convenience rather than shared ideology.

Conservatives may believe they can control or contain the fascist movement and use its popularity to maintain their own influence. However, this often backfires. Once the fascist leader gains enough support from the public and institutions, they begin to overpower their allies and use the legitimacy those alliances provided to seize control of the state.

In many historical cases, this stage marked the turning point from radicalism to mainstream power. The fascist movement benefits from the credibility lent by established figures, while those figures underestimate how dangerous their new partner really is. In the contemporary United States, this stage can be compared to moments when extremist or authoritarian-leaning groups receive support or tolerance from mainstream political actors. When politicians amplify conspiracy theories, excuse violent rhetoric, or form coalitions with anti-democratic factions for short-term gain, they reflect the same risky partnerships that once helped fascist movements rise in Europe. It is a reminder that enabling extremism for political advantage can easily spiral beyond anyone's control.

4. Dominate Institutions

This stage is when the fascist movement begins to dominate the major institutions of society, such as the government, military, courts, and media in order to consolidate control. At this point, the movement is no longer working from the outside of mainstream politics. It uses its newfound legitimacy and alliances to infiltrate and reshape the system from within. The goal is to replace democratic norms with loyalty to the leader and the party, ensuring that every major institution serves the movement's agenda rather than the public good, which sounds quite familiar to Americans in recent years.

The process often starts subtly. Fascist leaders appoint loyalists to key government positions, pressure the judiciary to favor their interests, and weaken independent oversight. They also target the media, labeling journalists as "enemies" or "traitors" while promoting propaganda outlets that reflect the party's goals. Over time, the institutions that once balanced power and protected democracy become loyalists, and they exist in form but not in function. When the military and police become politicized, and when public trust in elections and the rule of law breaks down, the fascist movement effectively controls the state.

In the U.S., this stage has parallels in ongoing efforts to undermine institutional independence. Attempts to delegitimize elections, politicize the justice system, and spread disinformation through partisan media all weaken the foundations of democracy. When leaders treat loyalty as more important than truth or competence, institutions become tools of power rather than protectors of the people. The U.S. has strong safeguards that make full institutional capture unlikely, but these warning signs highlight how fragile democratic systems can become when they are eroded from within rather than attacked from the outside.

5. Radical Reforms

This stage is when the fascist movement, now firmly in control of government and major institutions, begins to implement radical reforms that reshape society to fit its ideology. Having eliminated or silenced most opposition, the regime moves quickly to consolidate total power. The reforms are framed as necessary to restore the nation or protect its people, but in reality, they mostly dismantle civil liberties, suppress dissent, and enforce strict loyalty to the leader and party.

These reforms often target education, the press, and the economy to ensure complete ideological conformity. Schools are used to spread propaganda and glorify the regime's values. The media is censored or taken over to eliminate criticism. Economic and social policies are restructured to favor loyal supporters, while minority groups and political opponents are blamed for national problems and punished under new laws. What begins as reform quickly becomes repression, with violence and intimidation used to maintain obedience.

Currently in the United States, hints of this stage appear in the push by some political figures to rewrite history curricula, ban certain books, and restrict academic discussions on topics like race and gender. These efforts are often justified as protecting freedom or traditional values, but they reflect attempts to control public thought and limit open debate, which are tactics that have historically made authoritarian control much easier and more likely. While America's democratic framework remains strong, these trends serve as a warning of how easily reforms meant to fix society can become tools to silence it.

Clearly, reflections of fascist governments continue to show up in the U.S. today. The good news is that more people just like you are aware of it and are willing to fight against it. Fascist leaders, or leaders that want to be, despise knowledge about their motives among the people, because it robs them of their power. The U.S. is not currently in danger of becoming a full fascist state because of the copious safeguards in our democracy and constitution. However, the second we as citizens turn a blind eye to fascist characteristics and tactics in our government, we become highly susceptible to their propaganda and the state will get increasingly authoritarian. No matter the political party or ideology of a leader, they are there to be questioned. They are not infallible. They should have no loyalists; loyalism is the very principle that the Founding Fathers fought so hard against.

MULTIPLE PERSPECTIVES: THE ISRAEL-PALESTINE CONFLICT

The ongoing conflict between the State of Israel and the partially recognized State of Palestine is one of the most polarizing and emotionally challenging topics of our time. Fierce debates on this topic can be seen throughout the country and the world; on college campuses, in the media, and even around dinner tables. The problem is that these debates often reduce extremely complex issues to simple binaries. Behind all of the information and misinformation, the protests and riots, the nobility and the corruption, are very real people that are suffering and are in desperate need of peace. Peace cannot be reached if polarization continues to drown it out. Understanding the other side in a debate is one step in the right direction, and one step closer to adopting a peaceful resolution. The Israel-Palestine War does not just affect those in the Middle East; it is polarizing for American politics and has worldwide effects.[104] So, let us better understand how to interpret this conflict. A great way to do this is to gather multiple perspectives and compare, not just to rebut, but to genuinely try to understand each other. Note that the following perspectives are not necessarily generalizable to all supporters of either side, and the purpose of gathering information from one person from each side is to see if we can locate some common ground between people with opposing views that are both very far to one side.

---

[104] Mier y Teran, Anna. "War in Palestine and Its Impact on Western Countries." Global Affairs and Strategic Studies, University of Navarra, 20 Jan. 2024, www.unav.edu/web/global-affairs/war-in-palestine-and-its-impact-on-western-countries.

I asked one person who supports Israel and one person who supports Palestine to explain their respective viewpoints in a series of interview questions and see if there is any room for compromise or agreement. You can find the exact questions I asked at the end of this chapter. First, let us look at the perspective of the person who supports Israel. The reason given for their support of Israel is, "I support Israel over Palestine because I believe that Jews have the right to their homeland and country." However, their support of the Israeli people is different from their support of the government. "I don't support every action of Netenyahu but I do believe Israel has a right to defend itself. The people of Israel should be permitted [to] their land and the hostages freed." On the de facto rule of Palestine, they strongly oppose Hamas and its actions. "I think Hamas is absolutely committing human rights violations. They unpromptedly killed babies, dogs, women and men. They [rape] women. They took people hostage for being Israeli or Jewish, or in the wrong place at the wrong time. Israel is fighting a war. I understand why it hurts people to see what Israel is doing but at the end of the day they are in a war. [IDF] soldiers have to carry around a booklet in their pockets of rules to follow in order to make sure as [few] citizens as possible are killed. Hamas on the other hand doesn't care who gets killed, Gazan or Israeli[.]" They explain that in this regard, the blockade of Gaza is justified. "I think the blockade of Gaza is to protect Israel. Egypt has also blocked Gaza and there is no controversy around that. Israel has blocked them [for the protection] of Israeli citizens and Jewish lives."

So, what do Israel supporters believe is causing this conflict, and what does justice look like for them? "Antisemitism is at the root of this conflict as mentioned [before. Why] is Israel the only country we've ever called for the destruction of? Why is a Jewish state solution terrible? Why is harming Jews and repeating Nazi tendencies and ideals not being shown in the media? If the attack on [Boulder] was done during a pride parade there would be wailing in the streets. Why are [Jews] not being recognized as a minority and being targeted[?]" Generally, the issue according to this supporter is not the existence of Palestine as a state, it is anti-semetism and aggression by Hamas. In regard to this, justice according to this supporter is a peaceful two state solution. "I think the two should remain autonomous. I think a [two state solution] is important and Israel has a right to exist, [and so does Palestine] as long as they stop attacking [Jews] and Israel[.]"

Now, let us examine viewpoints from Palestine's supporter. The main question is the why: Why do they support Palestine over Israel in this particular conflict? The answer this supporter gives is that Israel has committed atrocious crimes against the Palestinian people without justification. They say, "Many people limit the conversation to everything that has happened since [October 7, 2023], but tens of thousands of Palestinians have been slaughtered by the Israeli government since the [beginning of Israel's] existence." On that date, the terrorist organization of Hamas attacked a music concert in Israel, killing hundreds of Israeli people.[105] Regarding this attack, this supporter generally believes that this was a tragedy and that sympathy can be held for the people of Israel, especially those who died in this attack or were taken hostage. They believe that it is important to acknowledge this as a terrorist attack while still holding Israel's government accountable for its actions in Gaza. A statement I found very powerful from this supporter about Hamas's attack was, "We can acknowledge this tragedy and hold sympathy for the people of Israel in this regard while also remaining aware that the Israeli government has been terrorizing the Palestinians for decades. There is no word to describe Israel's actions other than a genocide. It is not a conflict. It is not a war. It is a genocide." This is a common belief among supporters of Palestine, with many drawing parallels between Israel's military presence in Gaza and the Holocaust.

As for Hamas in general, this supporter is not a proponent of Hamas. They say, "To be clear, [Hamas's attack on October 7] was a tragedy. It is tragic that innocent Israeli lives were lost. It is tragic that innocent Israeli people were taken hostage."

This supporter also views this conflict as one-sided. "The Palestinians have no weapons. They have no defense. They have no food, water, healthcare, buildings, or any basic necessities. Israel has nothing to

---

[105] Estrin, Daniel. "Hamas Attack on Israeli Techno Festival Leaves at Least 260 Dead and Many Missing." NPR, 10 Oct. 2023, www.npr. org/2023/10/10/1204950063/hamas-attack-on-israeli-techno-festival-leaves-at-least-260-dead-and-many-missin.

defend themselves against," they say. The government of Israel is viewed as evil by this supporter, but they do not view the people of Israel the same. They do not view anti-zionism as the same as anti-seminitsm. Many view Israel's actions as war crimes; their statement was, "What they are doing is against the Geneva Convention. I can't stress enough how evil the Israeli government is." It seems that, for most Palestine supporters, the stress is on the wrong-doings of the Israeli government, and not the citizens that do not instigate violence. Let us now look at what events supporters of Palestine say could change their beliefs and cause them to support Israel instead. "Firstly, Palestine would have to rebuild at the very least to its former glory. Next, they'd have to accumulate massive amounts of weapons and their government would have to be fundamentally corrupt. Then, they'd have to start an endless barrage of bombings against Israel, for no reason other than imperialism and antisemitism. They would have to continue these horrible acts long after Israel became helpless. They'd have to target civilians and infrastructure. They'd have to commit atrocious war crimes and prevent Israel from receiving humanitarian aid," remarks one supporter regarding this. Essentially, it is the power dynamic that causes Palestine supporters to view Israel's actions as unjust.

So what do supporters of Palestine want to see, and what does justice look like to them? "I believe the West Bank and Gaza Strip should belong to Palestine. Additionally, I don't think the lines agreed upon in 1947 are very fair. I don't think Palestine was given an equal portion of land in terms of size and resources and additionally [I] don't think it's very historically accurate to where Palestinians have lived for millennia." This supporter essentially wants current Palestinian territories(Gaza and the West Bank) to belong to Palestine and be free of subjection to violence by Israel, and they want the territories to be redrawn, as Israel was given the more fertile land with generally better resources. However, they do not want to eradicate the State of Israel. They explain, "I think Israel has the right to exist as a state because it would be ignorant to pretend that [Jewish people never] inhabited that land. However, a [religious-based] ethnostate is inherently flawed and [only results in] further problems. A better solution would involve a [two-state system] that emphasizes human rights over religious differences."

Clearly, there is room for compromise and reform. Palestine supporters are generally adversaries of anti-semetism, believe in Israel's right to exist, and do not support Hamas or support the infliction of violence on Israeli people. Let us examine some similarities between both sides and places to compromise. First and most importantly, the situation that brings justice looks similar from both perspectives. Both people interviewed believe in a two-state solution where Israel and Palestine coexist peacefully as independent states and do not inflict violence on one another. Second, both are adversaries of anti-semetism and Islamophobia, which can often be perceived as the root causes of this conflict.

According to both perspectives, putting aside religious differences and peacefully coexisting in the region is the ideal resolution to this conflict. Third, both people want the violent actions taken by both Hamas and the Israeli government to end, and both agree that the events of this conflict are tragic. Fourth, both parties concur that the United Kingdom is at least partially to blame for tensions in the region, citing that the states of Israel and Palestine would have worked out a solution better without the input from the UK.

Let us quickly acknowledge the main disagreements between both perspectives. The main point of clash is the morality of Israel's military. While the supporter of Israel views the government's actions as defense more than anything, Palestine's support maintains that the actions of the government are evil. Beyond that, there are no major differences in their perspectives. That is incredible. This is debatably the most polarizing issue in the world today, and there was only one major difference between the two perspectives. Everything else was more or less agreed upon. These are simply perspectives from two people that I happened to interview, so they certainly do not represent the views of everyone who has an opinion on this topic. Nonetheless, it is an amazing feat to find so much common ground between two people that both lean heavily on their opinions, seemingly opposite. So next time you talk about this issue or another political topic with someone who shares a different opinion, keep this in mind.

Ultimately, if people share a common idea of a solution(a peaceful, two-state solution with no blockades or firing and the hostages made free), differences in opinions such as the motive of the Israeli government become completely insignificant. Let us not allow ourselves to become so polarized that we delay a solution long enough for human rights abuses to continue and governments to gain more power over us and their own citizens. We need to work together to hold global leaders accountable in order to stop actions like we all agree are terrible for humanity.

INTERVIEW QUESTIONS

For the interviews, I gave people two sets of questions, one for each side of the debate. I wrote more than one hundred questions but picked these questions specifically because I think that they are the most thought-provoking and require answers to be in-depth, and also to reflect on the views of the other side. I would encourage anyone that holds a belief on this topic to thoroughly consider your answers to the following questions, because, among other things, it helps you understand your own idea of justice in this context and keeps you from getting lost in the aggressiveness and polarity of the issue.

If you generally support Israel, answer these questions.

1. How would you describe the Israel-Palestine conflict in your own words?

2. In summary, why do you support Israel over Palestine in this particular conflict?

3. Is your support for the people of Israel different from your support for the government of Israel?

4. Has your perspective changed over time, and if so, what caused it to shift?

5. In your opinion, how has Hamas influenced the situation?

6. What is your opinion on the blockade of Gaza or the expansion of settlements in the West Bank?

7. Has the role that the U.S. has played in this conflict been overall positive or negative in your opinion? What about other western nations?

8. Do you believe that either side is committing human rights violations, and why?

9. What does justice look like in this context? In other words, what is the ideal outcome regarding casualties(civilian and army/ Hamas), statehood, and freedom?

10. How do you feel about the civilian population of Palestine?

11. Do you think the media portrays this conflict fairly? Why or why not?

12. What narratives do you see dominating your community, country, and the media?

13. If there was no conflict or violence from either side, would you be happy with how the borders have been drawn? Do you believe that the State of Israel should include the West Bank and Gaza, or should those remain autonomous?

14. What, in your opinion, are the biggest obstacles to peace in the region?

15. What role should everyday people play in supporting justice, peace, and awareness?

16. If you could go back in time and be an international law-maker just after World War II, would you have done anything differently from the arrangement that was decided?

17. What would the government/army of Israel have to do for you to stop supporting them, and even side with Palestine?

18. Have you done anything to work towards whatever goal you have for this conflict, whether that be two-state, one-state, or something else?

19. What do you think about people who support Palestine?

20. Does Palestine have the right to exist as an independent state in the regions that it currently is in, provided that it does not inflict any violence on Israel?

21. What is your opinion on Israel's attack on Tehran; was it justified? Has this changed your perspective on the conflict, and if so, in what way?

22. What is your opinion on islamophobia in general? What about as a method of resistance?

23. How do you believe religion has influenced this conflict; is it the sole cause or is there something else? Should it influence this conflict in your opinion?

24. Is there anything else you would like to add that you believe your full opinion on the conflict would be incomplete without?

If you generally support Palestine, answer these questions.

1. How would you describe the Israel-Palestine conflict in your own words?

2. In summary, why do you support Palestine over Israel in this particular conflict?

3. Is your support for the people of Israel different from your support for the government of Israel?

4. Has your perspective changed over time, and if so, what caused it to shift?

5. In your opinion, how has Hamas influenced the situation?

6. Do you support Hamas? If so, why, and if not, do you think its actions are at all justified?

7. Has the role that the U.S. has played in this conflict been overall positive or negative in your opinion? What about other western nations?

8. Do you believe that either side is committing human rights violations, and why?

9. What does justice look like in this context? In other words, what is the ideal outcome regarding casualties(civilian and army/Hamas), statehood, and freedom?

10. How do you feel about the civilian population of Israel?

11. Do you think the media portrays this conflict fairly? Why or why not?

12. What narratives do you see dominating your community, country, and the media?

13. If there was no conflict or violence from either side, would you be happy with how the borders have been drawn? Do you believe that the State of Palestine should include Israel's current territory or should it remain autonomous?

14. What, in your opinion, are the biggest obstacles to peace in the region?

15. What role should everyday people play in supporting justice, peace, and awareness?

16. If you could go back in time and be an international law-maker just after World War II, would you have done anything differently from the arrangement that was decided?

17. What would the government/Hamas/people of Palestine have to do for you to stop supporting them, and even side with Israel?

18. Have you done anything to work towards whatever goal you have for this conflict, whether that be two-state, one-state, or something else?

19. What do you think about people who support Israel?

20. Does Israel have the right to exist as an independent state in the regions that it currently is in, provided that it does not inflict any violence on Palestine?

21. What is your opinion on Israel's attack on Tehran; was it justified? Has this changed your perspective on the conflict, and if so, in what way?

22. What is your opinion on anti-semetism in general? What about as a method of resistance?

23. How do you believe religion has influenced this conflict; is it the sole cause or is there something else? Should it influence this conflict in your opinion?

24. Is there anything else you would like to add that you believe your full opinion on the conflict would be incomplete without?

VIGILANTE JUSTICE

In recent years, there has been increasing frustration with the police in the United States.[106] Some people cite incidences of corruption, ineffectiveness, or unjust and race-based murders as reasons for vexation. It is true, this country's police force and legal system in general is far from perfect and yields a copious amount of unfair outcomes. As an American, if an injustice occurs, you generally have three options: ignore it, attempt to correct it using this country's current system, or try to right the wrong by working outside of the legal framework. Correcting an injustice outside of the legal system is known as vigilante justice. So is it better to use the flawed framework that exists and potentially let the injustice continue or is it better to work outside the system and face the ramifications of that?

Let us examine two separate events that have happened in 2025 that demonstrate vigilante justice. First, the infamous(or not) shooting of conservative commentator Charlie Kirk. On September 10, 2025, a person allegedly unaffiliated with the U.S. government fatally shot Kirk.[107] Granted, suspected killer Tyler Robinson is currently in custody and has not been convicted of this crime yet. This sparked a huge controversy among Americans. Proponents of Robinson's action argue that he was hateful and his death removed this hatred, and that he is an extremely corrupt individual that lowers the quantity of life for Americans. They assert that since the system in place did not hold Kirk accountable, working outside of the system, or in other words, acting

---

[106] Cappetta, Jon. "Why We Hate Cops." High Times, 7 July 2023, hightimes. com/weirdos/why-we-hate-cops/.

[107] "Charlie Kirk: Trump Ally Shot at Campus Event in Utah." BBC News, www. bbc.com/news/live/c206zm81z4gt.

illegally, is justifiable. Adversaries of Robinson's killing of Thompson proclaim that violence is not a way to solve issues, and that murder is wrong, especially when the reason for the murder is an action taken by the victim within the boundaries of the law. In this case, Kirk's actions, no matter how morally questionable, were legal. Consider your opinion on this situation as you read the story following this one.

On June 14, 2025, a Minnesota lawmaker, Melissa Hortman, was shot and one was killed in a seemingly politically motivated assassination.[108] She was a pro-choice Democrat. Investigators believe that the suspect has a manifesto of seventy pro-choice Democratic lawmakers and allegedly it was a hit list of some sort. In the mind of the perpetrator, the murder of these lawmakers would save more lives than it would end, because of the pro-choice nature of their policies. She was murdered because of her political opinions and actions, and effectively had her voice violently suppressed by someone outside the government.

Now reflect on your opinions regarding both events. Was it justified for Robinson to kill Kirk?

Was the shooting of two and killing of one Minnesota lawmaker justified? If your answer to one of these questions is yes and your answer to the other one is no, it is probably because you are answering from a partisan standpoint. Partisan affiliation is a fine thing to have. Mostly everyone will have some sort of partisan bias. However, it becomes dangerous when your values change based on your partisanship. If you are against murder, but you condone it when it happens to someone you dislike or disagree with, you are not really against murder.

Since I do not believe in simply telling people what to think, I want to ask a few questions about vigilante justice for people to reflect upon. First, Kirk has indirectly condoned(multiple times) people's deaths for some reason or another.[109] If you celebrate his death, if you celebrate the demise of another human being, does that make you the same as him? If you are pro-life, you probably believe that Hortman also condoned killing. So, does celebrating their deaths make you the same as them?

---

[108] "Minnesota Shootings: Police Name Suspect." BBC News, 14 June 2025, www.bbc.com/news/live/cvgv4y99n7rt.

[109] "How Do We Talk about Charlie Kirk? : It's Been a Minute." NPR, 12 Sept. 2025, www.npr.org/transcripts/nx-s1-5538464.

ABIGAIL SAXEN

Second, "First they came for the Jews and I did not speak out because I was not a Jew..." and you know the rest of the poem. When you condone suppression of free speech for any single person, are you condoning it indirectly for everyone, even those you agree with? Third, who does suppression of free speech hurt the most? Is it white men like Charlie Kirk, and is it powerful politicians, or is it women, minorities, and common citizens? Who are you ultimately hurting when you condone suppression of free speech in its highest degree: violence? Fourth, what are you so afraid of that you feel that Kirk and the lawmakers had to die? Have authoritarian regimes in history risen to power because everyone, no matter their belief system, was allowed to talk and think freely, or have they risen because people were scared to say what they think because of the threat of violence? Fifth, when you condone gun violence in any form, what makes you different from the people you hate so much that you are celebrating them getting shot? Sixth, what atmosphere are we creating for people who want to go into politics, on any side? A welcoming or scary one? These are the types of questions that we need to be asking ourselves and others in order to create the best possible atmosphere for politics, so that more people want to go into the field.

CRITICAL THINKING AND STATISTICS

In the chapter on belief perseverance, I outlined methods to avoid falling victim to misinformation, extreme partisanship, and propaganda. In this chapter, now that you have read my examples throughout the book, I want to go deeper into that and talk more specifically about things I do in day-to-day life to have critical thought. To be clear, I have political beliefs, and I do lean to one side of the political spectrum. The point of putting your beliefs into question and avoiding belief perseverance is not to become a centrist. The purpose is to think about which viewpoints provide the greatest benefit, and which ones most align with your values; and once you do form political beliefs, to have the ability to change them in light of new evidence or understanding.

One thing that I do, and that I believe everyone should train themselves to do, is to be skeptical of everything, and I mean *everything*. Practice questioning things you hear that are not even related to politics. What if I told you that I killed an ant by throwing it off a tall building? How about if I told you I am sad because the dinosaurs were probably scared when the meteor hit? These are real things that people have said to me. Think about these statements for a minute. They seem quite plausible at first, but when you think about it, they do not make any sense. The mass of an ant is so small that gravity has almost no impact on it, so it cannot be killed by falling from a high point, and the meteor changed the climate and made it gradually unlivable for dinosaurs which is what made them extinct rather than the impact. These are light-hearted flaws in logic, but if you can train yourself to put these types of random statements into question and think "that doesn't seem right", you will be far less impacted by false statements or misinformation when it really matters.

Another major thing that helps improve critical thinking is learning that correlation does not imply causation. I see so many politicians from all sides of the political aisle attempting to get people to fall into this trap. This is the very first thing I think about when I hear arguments. Among Olympic athletes, those who eat more chocolate perform better than those who eat less. It is true. So if you want to be a good athlete, you better start eating lots of chocolate. Chocolate companies do not want you to think about the fact that chocolate is considered a luxury good, and richer countries eat more of it, while also performing better in the Olympics due to better equipment and resources. Chocolate will not make you a better athlete. Resources will. Train yourself to think about what is really happening. Biden's policies *caused* the economy to worsen. Or was it the aftermath of the pandemic? The very year that Bush became president, the World Trade Center attack transpired, so he must have *caused* it with his foreign policies. Or was it because of the years of brewing geopolitical tensions between Western governments and organizations in the East? Additionally, keep in mind that an experiment is the only way to prove causation. This is a study in which a variable is being manipulated by the researchers. If the correlational data is gathered from a study that is not an experiment, assume there is no causal relationship between the variables. I believe that truly understanding and thinking about the difference between correlation and causation will make us as citizens resistant to almost all political propaganda, because of how common this particular fallacy is, and how tempting it is to fall for.

Beyond correlation versus causation, understanding what makes a study valid and significant is a great way to think more critically about information. In a survey study, a sample size of at least fifteen hundred respondents is one of the requirements needed to make it generalizable to a larger population. If you are looking at a survey study that the researcher is attempting to generalize to a large population, and the sample size is smaller than this, discount the source. When analyzing a study, look at its p-value, which is a measure of statistical significance. If the p-value is higher than 0.05, discount the source. This means that the data found in the study is statistically insignificant and was caused by random chance. Look at the methodology of a study. Does the methodology yield truly random results, or is it biased? I once read a statistic that 97% of citizens from Ohio believe that voting is important to uphold democracy. First of all, since voter turnout is much lower than that, this seems suspicious. Second, the methodology yielded incredibly biased results. When I looked into the actual research, I found that the poll had around around two thousand responses, which is enough to not be discounted immediately. However, the methodology was that researchers stood outside of a polling location and asked the survey questions to anyone who would answer. People that are at a polling location are far more likely to believe that voter turnout is important, first of all. Second, people are more likely to answer a question if it is asking about something that they care about. This skews the data *heavily* in favor of people answering yes when asked if voter participation is important for democracy. This is not random sampling. The data is only from one polling location, and it is an elective survey. If a study has methodology like this, discount the source. Too often, I see research papers and journals get away with spreading bad data because people do not read or think about the context, statistical significance, or potential bias in methodology. Train yourself not to fall into this trap.

I am always extra wary of survey studies in general. Every year at my high school, every student is required to answer a survey about drug usage. Since every student completes the anonymous questionnaire, it does avoid bias in that regard. However, I always watch firsthand how everyone either selects arbitrary answers without reading the questions, or they write that they abuse hard drugs every day of the week when in reality they do not even drink caffeine. When we do that survey, I always wonder if the researchers realize how bad their data is, and if they are going to portray it as accurate, random, significant, and unbiased. I hope not; it is terrible and completely inaccurate data. This is a nonpolitical example, but this happens in polling data such as horse race surveys all the time. Be cautious about this. I have observed that most of the time, people are not intentionally being deceptive when it comes to presenting bad survey data from a seemingly legitimate study. By always questioning the methodology and potential bias of these kinds of studies, you can help prevent yourself and others from believing misleading or inaccurate data.

FINAL WORDS

Democracy is not a finished project. It was never meant to be. It is a living system that reflects the choices of the people that live under it. That is its greatest strength as well as the thing that makes it vulnerable. The genius of democracy is that it is a project that everyone can work on together. Use your rights. Not everyone has them. Keep questioning beliefs, no matter who they belong to. Train yourself to become a critical thinker. Call people out when they say or post propaganda, especially when they are on your side of the political aisle. Scroll past social media posts that do not mention a source. Join local and state elections that you care about. Sign up to be a poll worker. VOTE. At its best, politics is just about service. By fighting for what you believe in, you are doing a service to every American. The goal of politics is simply coexistence. It is about finding ways for all different types of people to live in the world together and have the highest possible quality of life. It may not seem like that in today's political climate, but that is ultimately what it is about. The next time someone tells you that they are not into politics, remind them of that. It is just a service to your fellow human beings, and that is all it was meant to be. Democracy does not work when people do not care to participate. With that, I want to restate a quote from one of my favorite authors: someone whose literary works contain much of the greatest thinking of our time if you pay attention. I believe this quote summarizes everything that democracy means, and everything it was ever meant to be. Unless. "Unless someone like you cares a whole awful lot, nothing is going to get better. It's not."-Dr. Seuss. If nothing else, I hope this book was for you an engraved stone tablet that reads, "UNLESS".

First and foremost, I would like to thank my parents for all the love and support. They have been my absolute biggest encouragers throughout the writing process and I completely owe my ability to write this book to them.

The rest of my family has also been huge supporters of mine throughout this process and I would like to thank them for all of the encouragement and backing.

I also owe a huge thank you to all of my amazing friends, not only for helping edit and revise this book, but for supporting me through the whole process.

Thank you to the candidates who graciously allowed me to work with them on their campaigns. You allowed me to make a difference despite being too young to vote.

I very much appreciate all of my teachers, coaches, and staff at my high school for supporting me and providing me with the skills necessary to write a book like this. Thank you to all of them.

A special thanks to my government, U.S. history, world history, statistics, and psychology teachers. Your classes helped so much with inspiration and knowledge for these ideas.

Thank you to the people who provided well-thought out responses to interview questions about contemporary conflicts. I could not have written this book without you.

Lastly but most importantly, thank you to anyone that has ever done something to keep the flame burning. Not just in the U.S., but across the world and throughout generations. That includes everyone who took the time to read this book. Every single one of you is the only reason I am even allowed or able to write and publish a book.

www.ingramcontent.com/pod-product-compliance
Lightning Source LLC
Chambersburg PA
CBHW022124280326
41933CB00007B/538